THE BLACK PRESS
IN BRITAIN

THE BLACK PRESS
IN BRITAIN

IONIE BENJAMIN

tb

Trentham Books

First published in 1995 by Trentham Books Limited

Trentham Books Limited
Westview House
734 London Road
Oakhill
Stoke-on-Trent
Staffordshire
England ST4 5NP

British Cataloguing in Publication Data
A catalogue record for this book is available from the British Library.

ISBN: 1 85856 028 4

Acknowledgements

Much appreciation and thanks to Onyekachi Wambu,
Herman Ouseley, Kolton Lee, Irene Shelley, Angella
Johnson, David Killingray, Hakim Adi, Marika
Sherwood, Chris Myant, Iqbal Wahhab, Abdul
Montaquin, Jacob Ross, Pearl Connor-Mogutsi, Nadia
Cottouse, Donald Hinds, Billy Strachan, Trevor Carter,
Elaine Sihera, C. Goodman-Olayinka, Tony Douglas,
Alfred Tang-Chow, Russell Pierre, Colin Prescod, Ralph
Straker, Voice Communications, Hansib Publishing,
Choice FM, Identity Television, The Gleaner, Azania B
and Alan Thompson, Johnson Publishing, Black Cultural
Archive, Rasheeda Ashanti, the BBC, the NUJ, Beulah
Ainley, Mike Phillips, Trevor McDonald, Hugh Muir,
Channel Four, BSkyB, Carlton Television, Colin Mabley
of East London University, John Bird, Tom Wengraf and
Mike Riddell of Middlesex University, Professor John
Eggleston of Trentham Books, John Stipling of
Trentham Print Design, Gillian Klein editor, S. Lyseight,
L. Jacques, C. Findlater, D. Afflick, M. Scott and
relatives and friends for positive support and to the
Creator for the inspiration.

Cover design by Shawn Stipling

Designed and typeset by Trentham Print Design Limited, Chester and
printed in Great Britain by Bemrose Shafron Limited, Chester

Contents

Foreword

by Trevor McDonald

The justification for the writing of this book is clearly stated from the outset. It is the fact that London is rapidly becoming the Black newspaper capital of the world. How London achieved this status is broadly the subject of Ionie Benjamin's *The Black Press In Britain*. It is without doubt a fascinating history, which by its very nature also touches inevitably on the evolution of sensible race relations in this country, the absolute horror, degradation and brutality of slavery, and the unending battle in the British colonies for self determination. If only for what it tells us about this, this is more than a useful study.

Although black writing existed in Britain as early as the late eighteenth century, the publication of black journals only gained momentum in the early nineteenth century. They were always of a campaigning nature. That they were had been dictated by the nature of the times. It is sobering to be reminded that there were serious race riots in Britain in 1919. Black servicemen who had helped in the ferocious battles of the First World War were denied the decency of being able to settle in Cardiff or Liverpool, with terrifying hostility, They were attacked in the streets and in their homes. Some were frightened away by this unconscionable mob violence, others stayed to fight and to launch the papers, journals and magazines which have now become part of the life of this country.

In this development, Benjamin's book reminds us of the sterling contributions of those great names, Marcus Garvey, George Padmore, C.L.R. James and David Pitt. They worked in difficult days and stern times, struggling to keep alive the liberal ideas they were determined to publicise not only in Britain, but through international affiliations, across the English speaking world.

The great debate in modern black publications is about the degree to which things have changed. It is an inquiry which to some extent may decide in part the future growth of black papers. My view, for what its worth, corresponds with that of one of the four black journalists on the *Guardian* newspaper, Angella Johnson. Talking about the greater involvement of black writers in mainstream British newspapers, and in my own field I may add in radio and television, Johnson says: 'I think as people come in with the experience and the educational background, bright black people will eventually get on... I hope'. So say all of us. It might diminish the stature of publications which came into being mainly because of the perceived under-representation of black people in the life and spirit of the country. But it is a prize worth the winning. And it should not be impossible in my view because we have now become a thoroughly multiracial society and nothing will change that now.

However, T.S. Eliott said somewhere about the enormous perils ahead for people without history. Put another way, the perils are even greater for those who choose to ignore their history. Ionie Benjamin's book about the Black Press in Britain will be an invaluable aid in making sure that we never do. It is to be commended as an excellent reference about the path we have travelled and a reminder of the milestones reached.

Chapter 1

SETTING THE SCENE

London is fast becoming the Black newspaper capital of the world. At the last count there were more than a hundred newspapers and periodicals owned and controlled by Asians, Africans and West Indians and published in Britain today, mostly in London.

Black publisher and journalist Elaine Sihera predicts that by the end of the 1990s, when the European trade agreement starts to take effect there will be more than four hundred Black newspapers and periodicals piling into our high street shops. This is bound to intensify the competition among publishers, who are ever in pursuit of lucrative advertisements and increased readership and sales.

A brief summary of the Black press in Britain reveals that Black journals emerged in Britain in the early nineteenth century but really started to multiply in the early part of this century. The fact is Black publishing existed before then in the form of prose. They were published in letter form in periodicals of the day rather as the work of Dickens, and collated and produced as books. *The Letters of Ignatius Sancho,* published in 1782, for example, had a first edition of over 1,200 subscriptions. Sancho wrote very much in the mode of Lawrence Sterne. Another author was the African slave Olaudah Equiano. Mary Seacole — awarded the same medals and accolades as Florence Nightingale for her effective hospital management and nursing of British soldiers in the Crimean War — published *The Wonderful Adventures of Mary Seacole In Many Lands.*

In 1817 a paper called the *Forlorn Hope* was published by Robert Wedderburn. Wedderburn was born in Jamaica to an African slave mother and a Scottish plantation owner, who, unusually, had the decency to ensure that his mixed-race offspring would not be born into slavery.

In 1778 at the age of 17, Wedderburn chose to settle in Britain. He soon collaborated with working-class radicals of the period to fight for freedom of the press and freedom of speech. He later brought out the *Forlorn Hope* with the help of the like-minded Richard Carlisle. They were gaoled for speaking out for freedom and for fighting for a free press and were actually the first in Britain to openly condemn White brutality against Blacks. In his book *Staying Power* (1982), Peter Fryer records that Wedderburn sent propaganda leaflets to Jamaica appealing to Blacks:

> Oh, ye Africans... offspring of an African... for it is a crime now in England to speak against oppression... I am a West Indian, a lover of liberty, and would dishonour human nature if I did not shew myself a friend to the liberty of others.

He warned the planters to prepare for a fight.

At the age of eleven Wedderburn saw his seventy year old grandmother beaten to near death and his pregnant mother severely beaten by a White man. Years later his anger was unquelled and in 1817 he wrote in his journal that he could not forgive the Christian White man, whom he called 'the silly European'. He openly condemned the system of slavery as a crime against humanity.

The anti-slavery campaigner, Fredrick Douglass lived in Britain from 1845 to 1847, lecturing and promoting his book *The Narrative of the Life of Frederick Douglass, an American Slave,* and returned to America after he raised enough funds in Britain to purchase his freedom. Back in America, he brought out a monthly journal, the *North Star.* This replaced the weekly *North Star and Liberty* founded in London in December 1847, to which Blacks were already subscribing in Britain. But the *North Star* only lasted four years, partly because the subscribers, didn't pay up.

Most of the papers which emerged in the early part of this century and the pre-War and mid-War era were equally forthright in their condemnation of racial injustice. Papers such as *The Pan African,* the *African Telegraph* and the *Black Man* were the mouthpieces of the political organisations that were emerging, and the voice of Africans in the Diaspora. But although most were radical there were a few which were considered liberal, for example the *African Times and Orient Review* and the *Keys.* It was the norm among Black writers and publishers in Britain throughout the period of Imperial rule, however, to ensure that Black news organs maintained an opposing voice and an editorial stance against colonial oppression.

After the War and in the pre-Independence years the long established *Jamaican Gleaner*, once considered the mouthpiece of the colonials in the Caribbean and actually founded in Jamaica years earlier, launched a British edition in 1951 to meet the demand of the increasing numbers of migrants from the Caribbean that began settling in Britain after the War.

If the *Gleaner* was considered right wing, the *Caribbean News*, which emerged soon afterwards, was the ultra left wing equivalent. The organ of the Caribbean Labour Congress, it was brought out in 1952 by London-based Second World War veteran, Billy Strachan, an active member of the Communist Party. This newspaper was considered so radical it was regularly banned in the Caribbean and its distributors imprisoned on grounds that they were subversive.

By the time Africa started to gain its freedom from colonial rule, beginning with Ghana in 1957, those active in the propagation of anti-colonialism knew that it was just a matter of time before the rest of Africa and the Caribbean would be free. They were unrelenting in their editorial attack against racial injustice. Newspapers such as the *West Indian Gazette*, launched by political activist Claudia Jones a year after Ghana gained its independence kept up its editorial campaign against racial injustice. By the mid-1960s most of Africa and the Caribbean was free of colonial rule and most of these news organs had disappeared.

The period between the 1960s and 1970s saw the turning point in the struggle and the early days of Independence. The growing number of Black journals, magazines and newspapers became available to the now increasingly segmented Black population. One journal which began in that era was *Race Today*. It was produced by the self-help organisations, Race Today Collective and the Institute of Race Relations, whose chair John La Rose, also founded New Beacon Books. Darcus Howe, journalist, activist and presenter of Channel Four series, 'Devil's Advocate', was the first editor of *Race Today*. The present director of IRR, Sivanandan, in his account 'Rebellion To Resistance' (1982), describes how the Race Today Collective emerged from the radicalisation of the research and advisory body, the Institute of Race Relations. Howe had a history of radical Black activism and had worked on a Notting Hill-based paper called the *Hustler*.

A number of pamphlets, newsletters, newspapers and journals appearing between the late fifties and the early seventies. Most were short-lived and not all were readily available. These included *Black Voice, Grassroots, Freedom News, Frontline, Black People's Freedom Weekly, Black Workers Action Weekly, Black Liberator, Link, Carib, Anglo-Caribbean News, Tropic, Daylight International, The Hustler, West Indies Observer, Afro-Asian-Caribbean News* and *Magnet*.

The West Indian World, founded in 1971, became the first British-based African-Caribbean weekly newspaper to be sold nationally at the news stands. It gave a platform and a voice to the post-Independence generation who came to Britain either in their formative years or as adults. The *West Indian World* spoke out against poor housing conditions, discrimination, educational issues, whilst at the same time tackling post-Independence issues in the former colonies. The political journal *West Indian Digest* was already in circulation, the *Caribbean Times* appeared in 1981, the *Voice* in 1982, *Black Briton* in 1991 and the *Weekly Journal* in 1992. Meanwhile, a wide range of glossy magazines including *Root, Chic* and *Black Beat International, Origin* and *Candace* became available on the news stands.

Like the *West Indian World*, the *Caribbean Times* was mostly read by settlers from the Caribbean interested in 'news from back home'. The

West Indian World, which lasted from 1971 to 1985, had no real competition throughout the 1970s, but by the 1980s critics began writing it off as a paper with a 1960s mentality that needed to move with the times. By 1985 it began to suffer rapid decline due to two main rivals, the *Voice* and the *Caribbean Times* attracting a wider readership including its own erstwhile loyal readers.

When the *Voice* came onto the publishing scene it made an historic break from the past. It was launched as a tabloid and said to be the 'voice of Black Britain', the first specifically to target young Blacks. This was an unusual step, since popular papers as a whole target social class rather than age group. As a popular tabloid, it was launched with the notion that it would appeal firstly, to readers likely to subscribe to the *Mirror*, secondly, that the core readership would be the 18 to 30s age group. Thirty-one percent of its readers are aged 15-24 and thirty-nine percent in the 25-35 age group. Other early papers were said to have failed to appeal sufficiently to the average non-academic young Blacks. According to their marketing director, the *Voice* readership is 300,000. The *Voice* emerged less than a year after the 1981 riots during 'Operation Swamp'. The riots started in Brixton and later spread to other areas throughout Britain. Other papers established in the 1980s and 1990s include the broadsheet *Weekly Journal*, with a core readership in the 25-45 age group, and the short-lived *Black Briton,* which succumbed to the rigours of publishing life soon after the *Weekly Journal* was launched.

There has been an evolution in Black glossy magazine publishing and choices fluctuated constantly. Currently the more popular include *Pride Magazine, Candace, Visions In Black, Artrage* and *Black Beauty and Hair,* all offering alternatives to a mainly young Black British readership. Also succeeding in the market are magazines such as *Root* and *Chic*, founded in the 1970s and 1980s respectively. They were influenced by popular American imports, such as the monthly *Ebony Magazine* and the weekly, pocket-sized *Jet,* though these target a broader economic band and age range.

The emergence of the Black press in Britain grew out of the demand for a representative voice, a voice that redresses the balance of the discriminatory mainstream media. One that addresses the social, cultural and political issues pertaining to their communities, which in turn helps to correct the imbalance both in the media and across the political and social spectrum and which counters the negative stereotype stories propagated by some mainstream news organs. Moreover, the Black Press provides employment opportunities for Blacks who want to enter media professions.

Most of the Black population think that they are not represented by mainstream media in the same way as their White counterparts and that if there were no racial discrimination there would be no need for a separate Black media. But by and large the mainstream media, in the past and still today, largely exclude Blacks from their decision-making processes. So all one gets is the journalist who from time to time prints a story affecting the Black community, which is, more often than not, about crime or immigration. Occasionally there is coverage of personalities like Black supermodel Naomi Campbell or chat show host Oprah Winfrey or the occasional coverage of sporting personalities, say Ian Wright or Linford Christie but even that is not done satisfactorily, nourishing, as it does, the old stereotyped notion that if it's entertainment or sport, it will fit into the stereotypical editorial pattern.

Now and then popular tabloids such as the *Standard* and the *Sun* will publish an in-depth Black feature which could be described as non-derogatory and non-sensationalist — always a welcome change from the usual negative stories — but it is far too soon to say whether things will change greatly. At the moment improvement is only marginal. Media critics are concerned that tabloids such as the *Daily Mail* have done little to foster good race relations but have instead focused almost exclusively on negative social issues, primarily about immigration or Black crime.

Professor Stuart Hall, in his book *Policing the Crisis* (1978), analyses some of the stereotypical reports in the national tabloids. He examines the *Daily Mail's* reportage on Black crime, arguing that newspaper headlines and stories have a great impact on their readers and can promote certain negative stereotype notions and prejudiced views in their minds.

Traditionally, tabloid newspaper coverage borders on tittle-tattle and resentment as opposed to the broadsheets' serious and analytical news construction. Liberal papers such as the *Guardian,* the *Observer* or the *Independent* attempt to present a balanced view and they do the occasional Black story. Whereas tabloid reporters, when they do present stories and features relating to the Black community, tend to reinforce existing negative stereotypical images. Nor do they eschew the sensationalist journalism which they have created over decades.

Yet Black people have an interest in the mainstream media and overwhelmingly subscribe to them. Researcher and founder-editor of the bi-monthly multiracial magazine, *New Impact,* Elaine Sihera argues that in ninety-five percent of cases, the media's portrayal of Black people is offensive. Black people who are paid-up television licence holders and loyal newspaper readers, she observes, are being bombarded with negative images of themselves in return for subscribing to such media. She says:

> It is an appalling fact that historically, Black people in Britain, like America, with which Black people are historically linked, have been historically excluded from their power sharing structure.

The contributions Black people have made to Western society, from the days of slavery to the present, have been exploited but not

documented or publicised in the same way as the contributions made by Whites. Only recently are the odd token historical Black figures being included in a few textbooks. I want *New Impact* to be a thorn in the flesh of the establishment. Its motto is 'To Serve One Nation'. It reflects a society which is racially mixed and which shares similar sets of aims, objectives and ideals.

Elaine Sihera

Readership figures show that in spite of the vast number of people who have an interest in the media, the type of news stories which appear in the nationals concerning the Black communities — which make up a significant part of the population and a highly significant part of their audience and readership — are inadequate and largely stereotypical. There are fifty- four million people in Britain, of whom more than three million are African-Caribbeans and Asians. Forty percent of the non-White population live in London.

According to figures from the big nationals, for example News International's marketing department, a vast number of African-Caribbeans and Asians read at least one national daily. The breakdown is as follows:

West Indian and African readership:

News of the World	-	179,000
The Sun	-	161,000
Today	-	15,000
The Sunday Times	-	48,000
The Times	-	21,000

Asian readership:

The Sun	-	159,000
News of the World	-	157,000
Today	-	32,000
The Sunday Times	-	75,000
The Times	-	37,000

(Figures for 1994)

Associated Newspaper Group, publishers of the *Daily Mail*, the *Evening Standard* and the *Mail on Sunday* was contacted to ascertain their readership figures but their marketing department said that they had national readership figures but no figures for Black readership.

Though Blacks are still so underrepresented — and misrepresented — in the mainstream media to which they so widely subscribe, there is nevertheless still some optimism that, with greater spending power than ever before and increasing population figures, a combination of the sheer Black population numbers and their stronger economic base will eventually force change in the mainstream, because economically, it will suit their purpose. But until changes are made, there will be people who feel they are not getting a fair deal and there will always be entrepreneurs who will want to describe their own activities as they feel these should be described.

In Brent, for instance, where forty-three percent of the population is Black, their consistent effort to broadcast through pirate stations highlights the urgent demand for substantial media representation. When the Broadcasting Act came into effect encouraging media franchising in the Thatcherite era, Black media entrepreneurs were given the opportunity to set up their own legal radio and television stations but it was hardly enough. Choice FM is still campaigning for a London-wide licence. Black newspaper and periodical publishing in Britain, on the other hand, not governed by the same constraints as broadcasting, emerged in the early part of the twentieth century during the era of British colonialism.

Chapter 2

THE PIONEERS

In the early days, Black owned and controlled newspapers and journals were nearly all affiliated to an independent or political organisation, all campaigning for the liberation of Africa and the descendants of Africa. The news organs put out by the new organisations articulated the woes and aspirations of the millions of Africans and descendants of Africans in Britain and around the globe, who needed a representative voice on a global scale. The Pan-African Association which published a news organ called the *Pan African*; the International African Service Bureau brought out a journal called *Africa and The World*, later the *African Sentinel*, and the West African Youth League produced a weekly paper founded by Wallace Johnson called the *African Standard*. Members and contributors were mostly students and academics who became political campaigners because the political climate left them little choice. They took the struggle to London, the heart of the Empire.

The *Pan African* was launched in October 1901 as the mouthpiece of the first Pan-African movement, founded in 1900. Those in the movement were among the most strident in their efforts against imperialism. Its founding President was a lawyer from Trinidad, Sylvester Williams. In 1900 he led a group of London-based Trinidadians to lobby MPs at the House of Commons on issues of British atrocities in the colonies. He was the first person of African descent ever to address MPs at the House of Commons. His humanitarian activities in Britain extended to campaigning work as a member of the Fabian

Society. In 1906 he was elected a local councillor in Marylebone Borough Council.

The board of executives on the Pan-African committee included the famous composer, Croydon-born Samuel Coleridge-Taylor, Gold Coast-born writer and lawyer, J.E. Casely-Hayford and J. Loudin, formerly of the Fiske Jubilee Singers. The PAC's first conference was held at Westminster Town Hall in July 1900 and attracted speakers from other parts of the world, including American educationalist, Booker T. Washington and political advocate, W.E.B. DuBois. A year later, Williams travelled to Jamaica, Trinidad and the United States to set up branches of the PAC.

When the *Pan African* was launched, its stated objective was to be 'the mouthpiece of the millions of Africans and their descendants'. Its contributors were uncompromising in their defence of Black freedom and the paper fought on those issues. It campaigned passionately for the Pan-African aims of self-determination, declaring that very little was known of educated Negroes and that it was time they set out to put this right. Nonetheless the *Pan African* was relatively short-lived.

The *African Telegraph*, incorporating the *African Journal of Commerce* was launched in 1903 by Sierra Leonean journalist and businessman John Eldred Taylor. It was a quality newspaper with a balanced perspective. It covered political, commercial and social issues pertaining to people, both Black and White, in Britain and the European colonies, in words and pictures. Explaining its aims and objectives and the reason for its existence the editor said:

> We are here because we ought to be... because it can be demonstrated that the African colonies and all that pertains to their social welfare have received scant justice at the hands of journalism... While we shall do everything possible to interest our English readers in the activities of Africa and the West Indies we shall at the same time strive to interest our large circle of African readers in the concerns of Great Britain and the Empire...

One issue published a critique of White stereotyping of Black Africa and how the term Africa conjures up certain images in the minds of a large section of the British public. To many, the piece observed, Africa is only a geographical expression, 'suggestive of wild and lawless hordes antagonistic to the influence of Western civilisation.' The *African Telegraph* was produced from the same office as the African News Agency, at Lincoln House, High Holborn, London.

The relatively liberal *African Times and Orient Review* was launched in 1912 as a Pan-Asian and Pan-African media organ by businessman and activist, Egyptian-born Duse Mohamed Ali, with the help of John Eldred Taylor. This was said to have been inspired by a meeting of the Universal Race Congress held in London a year earlier and attended by the Indian politician Gandhi, at the time the leader of the Indian community in South Africa. Also at the Congress was the Black American political activist W.E.B. DuBois.

The first news organ with a definitive Pan-African-Pan-Asian perspective and a conservative interest in commerce and industry to emerge in Britain as a voice for Africans and Asians in the Diaspora was the *African Times and Orient Review*. It could be described as both a Pan-African paper — it fought for the interest of Africans everywhere — and a Pan- Oriental one — it was concerned with the social and business welfare of Eastern people. It focused on the socio-political, cultural and commercial issues of what the West today calls the Third World and it had a certain amount of influence in effecting political change. It had set out primarily to tackle the major global political issue — colonialism — which affected both Africa and Asia at the time.

The *African Times and Orient Review* was a relatively moderate paper, although some of its writers took a more radical editorial line. The editorial staff consisted of a multiracial team of Africans, Asians as well as White liberals. The composer, Samuel Coleridge-Taylor, a consistent supporter of Pan-Africanism who in 1900 was elected to the executive of the Pan-African Association, wrote in the *African Times and Orient Review's* very first issue:

> There is... a large section of the British people interested in the coloured races; but it is... a commercial interest only. Some of these may possibly be interested in the aims and desires of the coloured

peoples; but, taking them on a whole, I fancy one accomplished fact carries far more weight than a thousand aims and desires ...

In support of the newspaper, he continued:

> ... it is imperative that this venture be heartily supported by the coloured people themselves, so that it shall be absolutely independent of the Whites as regards circulation. Such independence will probably speak to the average Britisher far more than anything else, and will ultimately arouse his attention and interest ...

In one edition, the Jamaican visionary and pioneer, Marcus Garvey wrote a thoughtful article on the subject of 'The British West Indies In the Mirror of Civilization'. He described how Jamaica became a colony of England in 1665 under Oliver Cromwell after they drove Spain out, and how John Hawkins obtained a charter to convey 'Negroes' from Africa to the West Indies. He wrote that among the many 'piratical and buccaneering heroes or rogues, whichever you wish to call them', were Teach, otherwise known as Blackbeard; Morgan, John Hawkins, Rogers, Drake, Raleigh, Preston, Shirley, Jackson and Somers, and that 'such terror did they strike in the hearts of their African captives...'

Garvey, himself one generation removed from slavery, bemoaned the inhuman treatment of slaves. They were beaten and tortured for the slightest offence and he describes one of the primitive methods of chastisement, which was to 'dance the treadmill', an instrument that clipped off the toes when not danced to the specific motion. He wrote that on many occasions the slaves revolted, in self-defence and revenge of such treatment, but with little or no success, because without military arms 'they were powerless in the face of organised military forces of the ruling classes.'

Garvey reminded readers that when a law was passed in 1834 declaring all slaves within the British empire free, twenty million pounds sterling was paid to the planters by the Imperial Government for the emancipation of the people whom they had taken from Africa but that the slaves got nothing. He wrote that 'they were liberated without money, property, clothing, food or shelter'.

The *African Times and Oriental Review* was situated at 158 Fleet Street in central London. Their offices doubled as a communal meeting place for the many African, West Indian, African-American and Asian students and activists that journeyed through London. The paper received some financial backing from share-holders. As Duse Effendi Ali reveals in a report, it was never enough. But despite the fact that the paper suffered periods of financial hardship it continued as a campaigning voice, reporting on the most pressing issue of the time, highlighting the sufferings of non-Europeans at the hand of Imperialists, throughout its publishing life.

The *African Times and Oriental Review* was well placed for attracting anti-colonial campaigners like Marcus Garvey, whose trip to Britain in 1912 was to be the first of many. For one thing, it was situated in the heart of London, the centre of the Empire's power base. Taking the struggle to the heart of the Empire, the campaigners formed lobbying organisations to strengthen their ranks.

The number of lobbying organisations continued to gain momentum. The African Students' Union was formed by a Sierra Leonean law student, E. Beoku Betts in 1916, and the African Progress Union two years later, for the furtherance of the interests of people of African origin. The APU consisted mainly of professionals and students of African descent and its founding members included Duse Mohamed Ali, John Eldred Taylor, of the journals *African Telegraph* and the *African Times and Orient Review*. Also involved was the Trinidadian-born London-based doctor, John Alcindor.

The inaugural dinner of the APU was held at the Great Eastern Hotel in London. Felix Hercules, Associate Secretary, proposed a toast to the 'African Race':

> There have been great civilisations in Africa. It is to an African people belongs the glory of the Pyramids and the Sphinx. In the South have been discovered the ruined remains of gigantic edifices that could only have been erected by a highly advanced people.

The constitution of the Union was to promote the general welfare of Africans and people of African descent; to establish a place in London where members might meet for political discussions and social activities; to spread by means of publications and discussion meetings the interest of Africa and people of African descent.

The first president of the APU was John R. Archer, who later settled in Battersea, considered a relatively militant London borough. He made history as the first Black Labour councillor, the first Black alderman and the first Black mayor in Britain. He was elected councillor of the Latchmere Ward in 1906 and mayor of Battersea in 1913. In 1931 he won Nine Elms ward and became deputy Labour leader of Battersea council. The national and local papers carried the story in their usual unrepresentative fashion. The national tabloid, the *Daily Mail* overlooked the fact that Archer was born in Liverpool of a Barbadian father and an Irish mother. The paper chose instead to promote the story upon Archer's 'keen contest with an Englishman'.

Archer's successor as President was Trinidad-born John Alcinor, from 1907 a district medical officer for 17 years for the Paddington area. Alcindor had attended the first Pan-African Conference in London in 1900.

In 1918, John Eldred Taylor, co-founder of the *African Times and Orient Review,* launched the *African Telegraph.* It was edited by Venezuelan-born Felix Hercules, who was also founder of the Society of Peoples of African Origin and associate secretary of the APU. By the following year the two organisations merged into the Society of African Peoples. Hercules was by mid-1919, secretary of the African Progress Union, following Robert Broadhurst.

It was the end of the First World War and Black seamen who chose to settle in Britain after the War and students from Africa and the Caribbean helped to swell the ranks of the growing number of Black campaigning organisations. The year 1919 saw some of the most serious race riots against Black servicemen in Britain, at Cardiff, Liverpool and other British sea ports. The Black War veterans were even barred from taking part in the Victory Celebrations on July 19, 1919. Black veterans all over Britain were attacked by marauding mobs in the streets and in their homes because of their colour. The Government stepped in, offering to repatriate the seamen to the colonies. Some took up the offer but many stayed to fight against the evil of injustice at the heart of the British Empire. The story of the riots was reported by the national and local newspapers such as the *Times* and the *East London Observer,* stating that homes were destroyed and individuals attacked.

But it was the Black papers which championed the cause, highlighting the ingratitude Black servicemen suffered, while the White papers understated the facts or apportioned blame. *The African Telegraph* reported in more graphic detail what the Black seamen were enduring, describing how Black residences were totally demolished and how men were brutally assaulted in the streets:

> They were drowned, butchered in cold blood and terribly maltreated and maimed... Every ounce of strength was put into the struggle by the Black man ... He fought with the White man to save the White man's home... and the War was won... Black men the world over are asking... What are we going to get out of it all?

The consequences of the War were to have long lasting effects on Black seamen in Britain. The Black organisations grew more vocal in their demands for freedom from colonial rule. Joint meetings were frequently held to discuss the future of Africans and people of African descent. By the 1920s Pan-Africanism became a force which gave the government much cause for concern. Twenty years earlier, the foundation for the Pan-African movement had been laid in London by such luminaries in the struggle as Sylvester Williams, the first person of African descent to speak in the House of Commons, the composer Samuel Coleridge-Taylor, West Africans Dr Ernest Jones Hayford and J.E. Casely-Hayford, and African-American Booker T. Washington, author of *Up From Slavery* and founder of the Tuskegee Institute. There were yet others such as W.E.B. DuBois of the National Association for the Advancement of Coloured People and Bishop Alexander Walters of the African Methodist Episcopal Zion Church.

In 1919 the Pan African Congress held a meeting in Paris organised by W.E.B. DuBois and attracting some sixty Black academics from around the globe. Speaker after speaker spoke out against the racist colonial regime and sought ways to end the sustained atrocities committed against Africa and the descendants of Africa. Although he was not directly connected with the PAC, Claude McKay, a Jamaican-born writer who lived in London for two years was prompted to pen the poem 'If We Must Die' for the journal the *Liberator.* He had first-hand experience of racism in the United States, where anti-Black rioting had also occurred two years earlier, and he articulated the Black man's burden. He wrote a letter of protest to the *Daily Herald,* which was refused by its editor and returned, but McKay was neither beaten nor bowed. He found a paper willing to publish it — the *Workers' Dreadnought* founded by a leader of the women's suffrage movement, Sylvia Pankhurst, as the mouthpiece of her Workers' Socialist Federation. Pankhurst offered McKay a job as a reporter on the paper and he became the first Black man to write for a White newspaper in Britain, until he returned to the United States in 1922.

The Black press in Britain brought out papers such as the *African Sentinel*, which came out in January, 1920. Its managing editor was T.H. Jackson. The paper was distributed by the Colonial Press Agency at 143 Fleet Street, London EC4 and published at the same address. It claimed to be 'the leading newspaper on African Affairs... representing advanced native opinion'.

On January 17, 1920 the *African Sentinel* reported that Marcus Garvey's Black Star Line: 'the SS Yarmouth, a 727 ton vessel which is owned and controlled exclusively by Negroes, left New York on its first voyage on 24th November 1919.' It called at Panama and arrived in Cuba on December 7th and in Jamaica on the 10th. The *Sentinel* noted that 'Captain Cockburn, a full-blooded Negro (late of Nigeria Marine Service) and the crew and officers' were members of the United Negro Improvement Association. The SS Yarmouth was later renamed the Frederick Douglas.

The article stated that the Black Star Line hoped to launch another ship — the Phyllis Wheatley — within a month or two and twelve in all within a year. The paper revealed that the capital of Garvey's company, UNIA, increased from $50,000 to $10,000,000 and that 'they hope soon to run a boat to West Africa.' It was at this point that the American authorities imprisoned Garvey and later deported him from the United States.

Black political groups included small bands of African students scattered around the country. There were African and West Indian student communities in university towns such as Edinburgh and Liverpool. Most sought to foster inter-racial-campaign links to further the cause. Delegates and representatives who were affiliated to political organisations with similar interests came regularly from overseas, protesting about conditions in their respective countries, all of them British colonies.

In August 1925 the West African Students' Union was formed by a Nigerian law student, Ladipo Solanke and a Sierra Leonian, Bankole Bright. Their initial objective was to provide support to African students and students of African decent. They set out to provide a base for these students to meet to discuss political, educational, economic and commercial issues affecting their countries. The Union was to play an important role in agitating for the end of colonial rule. In March 1926, the Union launched its own *WASU* journal. At first it promoted racial equality but it became progressively more radical, addressing the more pressing issues of African independence and the end of colonial rule. In 1928 the Union moved offices to a house which belonged to Marcus Garvey, and of which he had offered them the use. With money raised in Africa, Solanki opened WASU's first hostel in Camden in March 1933. A second hostel was opened in 1949 on Chelsea Embankment.

WASU held regular conferences, attracting influential Black radical members and White liberals. The further radicalisation of the Union came in the 1930s under the influence of George Padmore and Wallace Johnson, founder members of the International African Service Bureau which replaced International African Friends of Abyssinia in 1937. The Union was one of the scores of active voices of protest and they also provided a source of information through their newsletter, *WASU*. Every other Saturday members of the Union met in London to discuss West African problems, much of which was reported in their newsletter. Their organisation regularly attracted prominent politicians to their fortnightly meetings. In March, 1942, the day after the Atlantic Charter was pronounced by Clement Attlee, a member of Parliament visited the West African Student's Union. And at a meeting on 26 August, 1942, guest speaker Harold Macmillan donated £100 to the *WASU* and addressed some of the vexed topics, 'Mineral Reserves', 'Land Tenure', 'Forced Labour in Nigeria' and 'African Self-Government'

The 1930s saw the launch of campaigning newspapers and journals such as *The Black Man*; another *African Sentinel*; *Africa and the World* and the more conservative organ, the *Keys*. The International African Service Bureau was set up in March 1937 by Sierra Leonean-born political activist, Isaac Theophilus A. Wallace-Johnson, Trinidadians George Padmore and C.L.R. James, the Guyana-born Ras Makonen and Johnson 'Jomo' Kenyatta who was to become Kenya's first President. It replaced the International African Friends of Abyssinia, founded by C.L.R. James in 1936 in solidarity for Ethiopia (previously Abyssinia) after it was invaded by Italy under dictator Benito Mussolini. Ethiopia was one of only three Black nation still free from White Imperialist rule — the others were Haiti and Liberia — so its invasion marked a serious point in the Black liberation struggle. *Africa and the World* was established as the media voice of the IASB.

The weekly *African Sentinel* later replaced *Africa and the World* and was in turn succeeded by the monthly journal, *International African Opinion*. Edited by C.L.R. James, this was said to be a paper which aimed to bring African peoples closer together. But when War broke out in 1939 the Bureau became less active.

A journal called the *Negro World*, affiliated to the global movement, the United Negro Improvement Association, was the most successful Black news organ of its time. UNIA, a movement which at its peak was said to have up to six million members world-wide, was, like the journal, founded by Marcus Garvey. The vast international readership were mostly UNIA members from as far afield as Australia, America, Europe and Africa. Though UNIA's headquarters was actually based in Harlem in the United States, there were many loyal UNIA members and subscribers to the journal in various parts of Britain. Black students, political activists, writers and academics were at the forefront of the political and media campaigns. The Black media in Britain was born

C.L.R. James

out of that era when Black voices were suppressed and newspaper and magazine publishers were locked up in jail for selling and distributing Black newspapers.

At the heart of Black publishing pioneering was Marcus Garvey. He launched some six newspapers and journals during his relatively short life, and contributed articles to many others. He travelled extensively to promote his Black consciousness movement and his various news organs. He lived in Britain and elsewhere at intervals between 1912 and 1940. He was also founder of the biggest global Black movement ever, the United Negro Improvement Association, in Jamaica in 1914.

In 1910, at the age of 23, Garvey started his first newspaper. He travelled extensively, staying for varying lengths of time in the United States, Europe, Central America, South America and the Caribbean, working and setting up branches of his UNIA movement and UNIA groups, which also served as distribution outlets for his publications. Garvey's main mission was to preach the doctrine of self-determination, self-reliance and self-respect. UNIA's motto was 'One God! One Aim! One Destiny!' He moved UNIA's headquarters from Jamaica to Harlem, New York in 1918. He later established branches and outlets in London, Manchester and Cardiff and in almost every continent.

Garvey was to publish newspapers and periodicals in countries around the globe in English, French and Spanish and he was the first to publish a multilingual newspaper. His paper, the *Negro World* was printed in English with sections in French and Spanish and was the most widely read Black paper of its time. It was said to be feared by British, French and other colonial rulers. Accordingly, the paper was regularly banned in various French and British colonies including British Guiana (Guyana), Gold Coast (Ghana), Trinidad, British Honduras (Belize) and Rhodesia (Zimbabwe) but not Britain. Returning Black seamen played a part in helping their circulation, embittered by the treatment they received during the War. The paper offered them encouragement and hope and they were only too willing to smuggle the papers into the colonies.

Garvey's response to the bans was:

> I think the British Government made a great mistake when they suppressed the *Negro World*, because they only opened the eyes of those sleeping Negroes to a realisation that the government was trying to keep something from them, to keep them in darkness about the great progress of Negroes in the outer world.

Garvey launched other papers: *La Prensa* (The Press) in Panama and *Le Nacion* (The Nation) in Costa Rica as a voice of West Indian migrant workers. An evening paper, the *New Jamaican* appeared much later, in 1932. The *Black Man* was first published in Jamaica in 1929 and later published in London. The *Negro World*, founded in 1918, had subscribers world-wide and was most successful of all his publications. Within a few years of its launch it became the most widely distributed Black newspaper in the world and was published up to 1933. The front page of each issue of the *Negro World* usually carried a stirring message by Garvey which readers, mostly UNIA members and supporters, would discuss at weekly meetings, much as Christian followers might read the gospel and discuss it at a church service.

Garvey was born in 1887, one generation removed from slavery, in rural St Ann, Jamaica. He moved to Kingston, the capital, to work as a apprentice to the printer P.A. Benjamin. By the age of eighteen he was promoted to supervisor and by twenty he had co-founded a union and was appointed its representative. In 1910, he established his first newspaper, the *Watchman*. In Britain, Jamaica and other parts of the world where Garvey travelled, the papers became widely read.

Garvey travelled to Britain on several occasions, the first in 1912. In spite of the constant racial discrimination, newspaper bans, fines and periods of imprisonment that he faced, he got around and established links with political groups in London and regional areas such as Liverpool. Whilst in Britain he contributed to other papers, such as the *African Times and Orient Review*. He moved to the United States in 1916 and in 1919 launched his shipping fleet, the Black Star Line. A UNIA convention in Madison Square Gardens four years later attracted over 25,000 Garveyites from America and around the globe to listen to the fiery orator sound the rallying cry for African nationalism.

But Garvey was ridiculed and despised by his opponents. The National Association for the Advancement of Coloured People (NAACP) was founded in 1909 by liberal White Americans. The Reverend Robert W. Bagnall, one of its senior officials, called Garvey: 'a Jamaican of unmixed stock, squat, stocky, fat and sleek with protruding jaws and heavy jowls, small bright pig-like eyes and rather bulldog-like face.' The prominent African-American integrationist W.E.B. DuBois editor of the Crisis, the NAACP organ, poured scorn on him, describing him as 'A little, fat black man, ugly, but intelligent eyes with a big head ...' Garvey responded in the *Negro World*:

> W.E. BURGHARDT DU BOIS AS A HATER OF DARK PEOPLE Calls His Own Race 'Black and Ugly', Judging From the White Man's Standard of Beauty.

The integrationists launched a fierce campaign against Garvey and some say their actions influenced the government decision against him. The 'Garvey Must Go' lobby agitated for the disbandment of UNIA. They held public meetings and distributed literature denouncing him. Several of its members wrote to the attorney-general calling for Garvey's arrest and deportation. He was eventually brought before the Courts of Law in 1923 to answer various charges filed against him and, after a trial lasting four months, he was imprisoned in Atlanta. There was a world-wide campaign to secure his release and in Harlem 150,000 people held a demonstration rally. Before he could serve his full sentence, Garvey was released and deported to Jamaica.

Thousands flocked to welcome him back but the *Daily Gleaner*, a Jamaican paper run by wealthy estate owners, came out openly against his return, declaring it a matter of deep regret that Marcus Garvey had arrived back in Jamaica. The paper ranted about the many prominent Jamaicans who had welcomed him home and observed that:

> Kingston has reached such a level of degeneracy that there is no knowing what she will do... a new spirit has passed over the lower classes which has nothing to commend it except its ignorance ...

It was in that environment of racism and oppression that Garvey, like so many of his generation, carried on his work under colonial rule.

Ironically, activists found London to be freer than the colonies. Garvey moved back to London where he continued the struggle. He settled at 2 Belmont Crescent, West Kensington in London. He kept in touch with other Black political organisations, including the International African Service Bureau and African Friends of Abyssinia.

By now, Garvey's journals were floundering and the London-based *Blackman* was only published at irregular intervals, because it was poorly staffed, particularly when he travelled abroad on political trips. Like its sister publication, *Negro World,* it faced the added obstacle of being banned in some French and British colonies, because, like all Garvey's newspapers and journals, it spoke out openly against White domination. All suffered from inadequate funding although they still attracted subscriptions globally. His umbrella organisation, the United Negro Improvement Association, which had in 1920 attracted over 24,000 delegates and members to its political rallies, was also losing support. With Garvey banned from re-entering the United States, some of the members began to loose focus and breakaway factions emerged. Garvey continued with regular speaking engagements abroad, however, using the *Blackman* as a vehicle of communication to the members of UNIA nationally and internationally.

Garvey suffered a stroke in 1940 and a malicious reporter put it about that Garvey was dead. This report appeared in newspapers all over the world. Press cuttings of such cruel reports flooded his office over several days, and this was said to have hastened his death. He died in London a month later at the age of 52, after another massive stroke, leaving his widow Amy to carry on the struggle and his legacy, Garveyism.

Garvey was a key global figure in the struggle against colonialism. He travelled the world with a mission to uplift the Black race and he started a newspaper at almost every mission post. The six newspapers and journals he founded in his lifetime played their part in the struggle. He infused a new soul into the lives of the Black people of his time and reflected this in his publications. He invoked a spirit of independence and propagated the message of self-respect among Africans in the Diaspora.

There was a global revolution of thought in the time that he lead the United Negro Improvement Association. It became a world-wide movement attracting six million Garveyite followers, in Africa, Europe, Australia and the Americas. It was the first time in history, since Africa was abducted by the West, that one man had won the respect of so many prominent academics and political activists world-wide.

Black people in the Diaspora saw him as a messianic figure-head; they learnt to trust and appreciate his political ideals and methods. They had faith in his sincerity and devotion to the good of the African race and acknowledged the contributions he made to the advancement of his race, despite numerous political set-backs.

The West African Students Union, formed in 1925, moved later to a house provided by Garvey, who had strengthened ties with WASU during his stay in London. Its founder, Lapido Solanke, and other students such as Kwame Nkrumah and Jomo Kenyatta had long been Garvey admirers. Kenyatta, who was studying at London University, actually lived in the house for a time. The first editor of WASU's newsletter, *WASU* was Dr E Udoma. The magazine dealt with the interests of students based in Britain and Ireland. Prior to the launch of the West African Students Union, Blacks were being attacked on all fronts: in the colonies and at the heart of the Empire. A colour bar was in full operation. Yet only a few years earlier, at the outbreak of World War I, thousands of Black men had responded throughout the Empire, to 'the Call For King and Country'. Black servicemen were posted in Europe during the First World War, and some returned to Britain after the War.

The Union met every other Saturday to discuss West African problems. At a meeting on August 26, 1942, the guest speaker was Harold MacMillan, there to discuss Mineral Rights, Land Tenure and African self-government and Forced Labour in Nigeria. In Kenya, for example, Africans were denied freedom of speech, freedom of the press and freedom of assembly. It was a criminal offence for more than five persons to meet together without permission. Every African had to carry a fingerprinted pass. Africans were not allowed to own land; the best land was taken away from them and allotted to White settlers. Such were the concerns of WASU.

Other lobbying organisations following on the heels of the West African Students Union included the West Indian Students Union in 1931, which started out as an inter-social group but later evolved explicit aims of opposing discrimination. Like the organisations themselves, their newsletters, newspapers and journals were to play a significant part in the struggle. They informed members of issues affecting them from around the globe. Most of the prominent Black political activists and students were influenced by Marcus Garvey. Some of them, on returning to their homelands to take up positions as political leaders, named public places and buildings after him. When Ghana became independent in 1957, for example, its first president, Kwame Nkruma, a life-long Garvey admirer, who had attended UNIA meetings while in the West, named Ghana's first shipping corporation after Garvey's 'Black Star' Line. Likewise, Nigeria's first Governor General, Nnamdi Azikiwe, in his acknowledgement and appreciation of Garvey, invited his widow, Amy Jacques Garvey to Nigeria to his inauguration in November 1960.

Statues have been unveiled in Garvey's honour in various parts of Jamaica. In New York in 1972 a ground breaking ceremony marked the start of a $200,000,000 urban project, called the Marcus Garvey Park Village. There was a commemorative stamp in Cameroon in 1969, and in London a plaque was erected in 1972 in his honour at his former offices in West Kensington and a $7,000,000 Marcus Garvey Gardens housing project in Boston in 1979. The Rastafarian movement was largely inspired by Garvey.

Garvey's remarkable success was based partly on his great skill as a communicator of both the written and the spoken word. A great visionary, Garvey realised that one of the most effective ways of getting a message across was through print and the spoken word, so he brought out newspapers in most of the countries where offices of UNIA were established and, as a gifted orator, he regularly visited those countries, spreading his message.

Chapter 3

THE LEAGUE OF COLOURED PEOPLES

Members and sympathisers of organisations who identified with the struggle for liberation from colonialism, were loyal subscribers to the Black press of this period. The newspapers and journals were distributed at the organisations' meetings or mailed to subscribers. As the media mouthpiece for these organisations, they effectively communicated news and information to Africans and descendants of Africans in Britain and around the globe. Most of these organs survived solely on subscriptions and donations. The multiracial organisation, The League of Coloured Peoples was founded in 1931 by Harold Moody and its affiliated journal, the *Keys*, in 1933. The *Keys* started out as a quarterly newsletter, to communicate news and information which affected Black people, to its members and supporters. The LCP regularly held fund-raising activities to promote its cause.

Harold Moody came to London from Jamaica in 1904. He trained at Kings College, excelling in obstetrics and clinical medicine but he failed to get a job as a hospital doctor because of his colour and became a family doctor instead. He practiced in Peckham, South London for over 30 years and was also a lay preacher in the Congregational Church. He, like most of his contemporaries, suffered racial discrimination on all fronts and, worst of all, in gaining employment and finding a place to live. It was in this climate of racial discrimination that the Black voice gained momentum in Britain. As the Commission for Racial Equality

does today, the League of Coloured Peoples took up cases in the 1930s of Black people who were discriminated against, particularly in the field of employment. Many hospitals, for example, refused to train or employ Black nurses.

The LCP was very much an interdenominational, multiracial organisation, attracting middle-class White liberals, students and servicemen. Dr Moody mobilised League members to attend rallies, conferences and seminars throughout Britain and to promote the struggles of Africans and people of African decent. The League had a board of seven Officers and thirteen Executives, all of them professionals and academics from various parts of the world who were living in Britain at the time. The founding executives included West African lawyers Stephen Thomas, Alex Koi and Stella Thomas; several Americans and Asians and several from the West Indies, including C.L.R. James.

During the economic depression in the 1930s, various public service and charity activities were organised by Dr Moody in association with the League. These included regular day trips to the coast and the countryside for Black children from poor families, and sponsored holidays and educational courses for students from Africa and the West Indies. The League held regular members' functions at Memorial Hall in London as well as bazaars and fêtes to promote cultural and racial equality and raise funds for their organisation. They attracted exceptional sports personalities such as the West Indian cricketer, Leary Constantine, who was a representative in the League's decision-making arm, the Board of the Brains' Trust. Singer, actor and lawyer, Paul Robeson gave a moving address on 'The Negro in the Modern World' at one Annual General Meeting.

It was said of the League's annual political conferences that, 'plebeians and patricians found a common ground'. Its main aim was to protect the civil rights of Africans and people of African descent. The League's stated objectives were:

Opposite:
Harold
Moody

- To promote and protect the social, educational, economic and political interest of its members.

- To improve relations between the races.

- To co-operate and affiliate with organisations sympathetic to coloured people.

- To render such financial assistance to coloured people in distress as lies within its capacity.

C.L.R. James, author of *The Black Jacobins, The Life of Captain Cipriani, Crown Colony Government in the West Indies, Beyond the Boundary* and many other books, was a founder member of The League. Addressing its first weekend conference in March 1933, on the topic, 'The West Indian', he asserted that 'Black man in the West Indies has been shorn of all African civilisation and that they have been engulfed by Western civilisation.'

Other conferences attracted such speakers as Jomo Kenyatta, later the first leader of Kenya after its independence, and Doctor Hastings Banda who was a student in Britain and later practiced medicine in Liverpool, where he was appointed president at the inaugural meeting of the Liverpool branch. He was also a member of the British Committee, the campaigning arm of the LCP which lobbied Parliament.

With the outbreak of World War Two, paper rationing reduced the *Keys* to a shortened typewritten version called *News Notes*. Doctor Moody tirelessly carried on campaigning, while five of his six children were in active service: his sons Captain Arundel Moody, 1st Caribbean Regiment; Lt. H.E. Moody, Indian Command; LAC Ronald Moody, Italian Regiment; A.C Garth Moody, based in Britain and his daughter Captain Christine Moody, Staff Surgeon in the Indian Command. On 8 April, 1942 Harold Moody wrote to the Director of the BBC protesting the omission of West Indians and Africans from their programme 'Good Night to The Forces' while acknowledging most of the other nations fighting in the Allied cause during the Second World War. By the 21st April Moody got a reply from the Director General informing him that West Indians were now included.

Affiliating *The Keys* to its largely middle class multiracial organisation, the LCP, provided it with a ready readership. It was sold almost entirely by subscription and copies usually sold out. Its readers would sometimes write in for extra copies. It was later produced monthly. One appreciative reader wrote: 'Please send me one dozen copies of the May newsletter, you are going from excellent to excellentissimus.' Another, from Sierra Leone wrote: 'It is a splendid newsletter, a regular mine of information, keeping its fingers on the pulse of all the problems confronting coloured people the world over'.

Donations were regularly received from various sources, for example: £20 from Vicountess Simon on behalf of a friend, £5 from Lord Faringdon and repeated gifts from Lord Olivier, as acknowledged by Moody in his letter in the editor's column in the January 1942 edition of *The Keys.*

Like the LCP itself, the *Keys* championed the cause of Black people. Some of the contributors who wrote articles were politically active League members and guiding lights in the struggle for liberation. Some were students and academics, others potential world leaders who joined forces with the 'movement' and later became President of their countries, for example, Kwame Nkrumah of Ghana and Jomo Kenyatta of Kenya.

Editorial contributions came also from other newspapers from around the globe such as *The Demerara Tribune, The India, The Lagos Daily, The West Indian.* Some of these provided world news about African people and people of African descent.

Much of the news reported in the White owned newspapers about Blacks was unfavourable, so when the occasional acceptable Black story did appear, it provided a welcome change and the Black newspapers would reproduce it. A typical story reported in the *Keys* concerned the Commonwealth Minister of the Interior, Mr Perkins and his announcement of the Government's decision to establish special 'Native' Courts to try Aborigines charged with offences. This had been extracted from the *Daily Herald* (22.6.1934). The same article reports one constable as having shot 43 Aborigines.

Another story, this time from the *Daily Mirror* of 8th June, 1940, under the heading: DUG OUT BOMB MADE IT SAFE was about a German delayed action bomb which had been buried in the garden of a house in a Welsh town. The report stated that a West Indian coloured soldier dug down to the bomb and made it harmless. The soldier, who said he had done similar tasks in France, volunteered for the hazardous operation. His commanding officer's permission was asked for and granted.

> People were cleared away from the neighbourhood and the soldier, helped by comrades forming a 'suicide squad,' dug a narrow hole six feet deep. He was out of sight when he reached the bomb, which he made harmless before bringing it to the surface. The people of the neighbourhood were so impressed that they made a collection of £10 and presented it to the soldier. He shared it with the comrades who helped him. A police officer who was standing near the scene of the operation told *The Daily Mirror*: 'The soldier had nerves of steel. He was as cool as if he was merely digging out a drain'.

Other Black news organs world-wide were also providing news. An African-American monthly called *The Crisis*, the NAACP's organ edited by Dr W.E. DuBois, provided many of the news reports of global interest which were then reproduced in the *Keys*. When the Commission on Inter-Racial Co-operation in Atlanta published a report on lynching statistics in the United States, the *Keys* reported it, revealing that more than 5,000 lynchings had occurred in the USA since 1892, of whom over 1,500 victims were White and 103 women. It also revealed that in 99.2% of the lynchings nothing was done to apprehend or punish the lynchers, and commented that America was the only nation on earth where lynching occurs.

But not all the stories were negative. The newsletter brought to the attention of the readers that it was an Afro-American who invented the machine gun. The *Evening News* on November 19, 1940, had announced that '... a negro has invented a 10-barrel machine gun and offered it to the USA Army.'

The Keys reported a speech by the scientist Albert Einstein, in which he identified the anti-imperialist struggle in Africa as 'a part of the world-wide struggle now being waged by minority groups to preserve their own cultural heritage, and to keep alive the remnants of democracy'. Dr Einstein gave this brief but moving speech after he heard Walter White, Secretary for the National Association For the Advancement of Coloured People (NAACP), the oldest civil rights organisation in America, address the second 'Inter-racial Good Will Hour', in April, 1940 at Princeton, New Jersey. Einstein was there to support the topic of the meeting: 'The struggle of the Negro people of America for full citizenship rights.'

When Marcus Garvey died in 1940, Dr Moody wrote a moving tribute in the *Keys*. He described how, as the President-General of the Universal Negro Improvement Association, Garvey conceived the idea of setting up a negro state in Africa and as part of this plan started the 'Black Star' Line — a line which was to provide transportation for Africans in the Diaspora to return to The Motherland — Africa. He acknowledged that Garvey was not a financier and, furthermore, was badly advised and disagreed with those who might have helped him. Although Garvey's activities had brought him into conflict with the American Authorities and he was imprisoned and deported, Moody declared that:

> Garvey was truly one of the greatest men the group (LCP) has ever thrown up. No other man operating outside of Africa has so far been able to unite our people in such large numbers.

Ken Campbell, a former editor of the *West Indian Digest* suggests that:

> *The Keys* was not just in the Caribbean interest in relation to Britain but it included India, Africa and America. If we were to look at the publications worked on by Dr Moody and leading figures of the age such as Marcus Garvey we do not see a compartmentalisation between the outer boundaries of the British Empire and the centre of the Empire. Compared with journals today which play on the sentiment, the journals of Moody's and Garvey's time were not looking at the internal market. In my own experience many of the journals such as Moody's were taken up with the anti-colonialism movement.

The LCP's campaigning work achieved positive results. In response to protests from the League and organisations which shared their ideals, they campaigned jointly with like-minded Africans and advocates to prevent the British Empire Games (now the Commonwealth Games) from taking place in South Africa in 1940 and forced them to be moved to London.

Moody's approach was to seek to promote peace and to break down barriers, forging links with religious orders and youth organisations and independent trusts and progressive people. Dr Moody's aim in association with the LCP was to secure equal opportunities for all.

The LCP had regional offices in various parts of Britain. The South-West Regional Office, for example, was based at Tavistock Road in Plymouth, the *Keys'* editorial office at 164 Queens Road in Peckham. The paper survived solely by subscriptions and donations and without advertisements and continued publishing well into the 1940s, and the organisation which Moody founded at the YMCA Hall in London, back in 1931 continued to gain momentum.

Doctor Moody died on 24 April, 1947 and at his funeral in Camberwell thousands of people paid their respects .

Like other journals of its kind the *Keys* was in great demand because it was a campaigning organ which championed the Black cause and reported stories different from the mainstream newspapers. Above all, it was a leading light in a political climate of anti-colonialism and in the struggle for liberation, a media voice for Black people around the globe who were unrepresented by the mainstream media which largely supported colonial ideology and ignored most events which affected the Black population.

Harold Moody was considered relatively moderate or even conservative and the organisation which he founded was made up largely of the academic elite of all races, so it escaped the constant harassment which the radical Pan-African organs endured, where people who sold or distributed Black campaigning newspapers and journals could be thrown in jail for 'anti-colonial activities'. All this happened in an age of publishing innocence and altruism, unlike the current climate of Black media competitiveness in the 1990s in Western society. Now that we have more freedom: freedom of speech and of the press, media competition governs.

Chapter 4

A NEW BLACK AUDIENCE

The seeds were sown for economic growth and increased political mobilisation among Black people in Britain after the War. The immigration pattern altered when the post-War boom created a climate for the recruitment of Black labour from the Caribbean. Caribbean-based papers such as the *Jamaican Daily Gleaner* helped to put the word about in the Caribbean that Britain needed manpower. A British weekly edition of the conservative organ, the *Jamaican Daily Gleaner* was launched in London in 1951. Its conservatism earned it the nickname, 'the *Times* of the Caribbean'. Its launch was timed to coincide with the increasing West Indian population, to meet a growing demand from new immigrant settlers desirous of 'news from back home'. Its owners and controllers were White Jamaicans planters. The early editions of the paper carried stories and news with a conservative perspective but over the years it has changed editorially, though it is still perceived as a conservative paper.

Post-war Britain under a Labour government was a time of austerity because rationing was still more or less the norm, but when the Conservatives came to power in 1951, they claimed to herald an age of affluence in which a war-weary generation who had experienced long periods of scarcity and longed for a better life would enjoy an improved economic climate.

Some Blacks who fought in the War had stayed on in Britain and others came to study. Many of those recruited from the Caribbean came from the 'British colonies' — Barbados, Jamaica, Trinidad, Grenada, Antigua and Guyana — to work in the service industries, particularly in the health service and public transport system in jobs the Whites did not want. The League of Coloured Peoples still existed up to the mid-1950s and continued to attract professionals and intellectuals with strong political convictions. Dr David Pitt (Lord Pitt of Hampstead), a Grenada-born general practitioner, was its Chairman, at new offices at 3 Robert Street off Hampstead Road in north-west London.

In 1952 Billy Strachan, a Jamaican-born member of the League and also of the Caribbean Labour Congress founded in Barbados, launched a monthly newspaper called the *Caribbean News*. Strachan was also at the forefront of a campaigning group, the Seretse Khama Fighting Committee which he set up with cricketer Leary Constantine in 1948. Seretse Khama, heir apparent of Bechuanaland (Republic of Botswana), had arrived in Britain to do post-graduate studies at Oxford University. He later married his English secretary, Ruth Williams, and the story made the national and international headlines. Because of his inter-racial marriage he was forced to give up his chieftainship and go into exile. The British government decision created public outrage. One of the first letters of protest came from E.A. Boateng, president of the West African Students Society at Oxford.

West Indians in Britain have always been at the forefront of campaigning for a just cause and many of them joined ranks with Leary Constantine, president of the Committee and Billy Strachan, its secretary. On March 12 1950, the SKFC held a meeting of protest at Dennison Hall, Vauxhall Bridge Road attracting over 800 supporters.

By July 1st, 1952 a second group was set up, mostly of parliamentarians from all three Parties. Its Chair was Fenner Brockway, the founder of the Movement for Colonial Freedom, and the Vice-chairman was Jo Grimmond. Labour MPs included Anthony Wedgewood-Benn and Conservative members included Quintin Hogg and Boyd Orr. David Astor, owner of the *Observer* newspaper and friend of Tshekedi Khama, Seretse's father, also supported the group.

Commenting on the party political group, Billy Strachan said:

Seretse Khama would pick me up four times a week and book me in at the Dorchester Hotel to meet and plot how to publicise the situation, how to lobby the British government not to acquiesce with the South African regime and this went on for several years.

Strachan was a Flight Lieutenant in the Second World War and was shot down over enemy territory, suffering severe injuries. Because of his Communist interests and his military background, *Private Eye* magazine described him as a 'veteran Communist Party hack'. During the War Strachan made propaganda broadcasts for BBC radio, on the programme *Caribbean Calling*. Yet in spite of his heroism in the war against Nazi Germany, he, like fellow servicemen, experienced racial discrimination when seeking suitable employment back in Britain once the War was over. He later trained as a barrister.

If the British edition of the *Gleaner* was perceived to be right wing, the left wing answer was the *Caribbean News*. Billy Strachan was an active member of the communist party, who had suffered periods of imprisonment for his political beliefs, and all the correspondents on the paper, including its editor, the Guyanese political activist, Ranji Chandisingh, were communists. Its youth correspondent, Trevor Carter, who joined the paper in 1954, says:

> It is a fact that all the writers on the Caribbean News were Communist. The editor, Ranji Chandisingh, eventually went back to Guyana and became Vice-President under Forbes Burnham's government.

Because of the writers' political activities and ideologies, the *Caribbean News* was banned in all the Caribbean islands. Editorially, the paper focused on news which appealed to its communist sympathisers and members nationally and internationally and openly condemned colonial rule and advocated Pan-Africanism.

In 1956, the political activist and journalist, Claudia Jones, who had arrived in Britain a year earlier, took over running the *Caribbean News.* Born in Trinidad, she had suffered excessive periods of imprisonment in the United States during the McCarthyite era of anti-communist activity — between 1948 and 1955 she served four long periods in prison. Finally released after mounting campaigns in her support, she suffered a spell in hospital due to a heart condition and was promptly deported to Britain where she tirelessly carried on her campaigning. On the subject of her contribution, both Trevor Carter and Billy Strachan stressed the wealth of experience and knowledge that she brought to what had already been achieved in the paper.

According to Trevor Carter:

> Claudia came with this history of experience from the United States after years of struggle. The period we were going through is something she had gone through years earlier; so she had the ability to transform what was an editorially narrow newspaper, which was seen as a leftist, subversive paper, into a popular paper.

But after Claudia Jones joined the paper not one issue appeared for a year because of internal wranglings and it was 1958 before she eventually brought out another: a weekly newspaper called the *West Indian Gazette*. She launched it with the help of Amy Garvey, widow of Marcus Garvey, at St Pancras Town Hall, throwing a party to bring the Black and White communities together. Among the Black celebrities who supported the event were Pearl Prescod; actresses Corinne Skinner-Carter and Nadia Cottouse, Pearl Connor, theatrical agent and co-founder of the Unity Theatre and Guyana-born war veteran and actor, Cy Grant. The launch party was televised by the BBC and that party turned into an annual street event. It was Claudia Jones who started the Notting Hill Carnival, today the biggest annual street festival in Europe. The Carnival is held every August Bank Holiday Weekend, culminating in two days of dancing, music and spectacle. It attracts over a million revellers and spectators — Black and White — from all over the world.

The Black population in Britain increased steadily from the late 1950s. Those who came as volunteers during the War were followed by others recruited to provide manpower in the aftermath of the War, and they in turn brought over their wives and children. The late 1950s were reminiscent of 1919, when social tension and unrest blew up after the First World War into full-scale race riots in the streets of Britain. Only it was much worse in 1919 — described as the worst riots in British history, when Whites all over Britain attacked Africans, Arabs, Portuguese, Chinese, Indians and anyone they perceived to be non-White foreigners.

In August 1958, rioting by Whites erupted yet again against Blacks. This time they started in Nottingham and, a week later, exploded on the streets of Notting Hill Gate in West London. Though not as ferocious as the events of 1919, they nevertheless gave the government an excuse to strengthen the Immigration Law, first passed in 1905 to keep out Jews fleeing the Pogroms in Eastern Europe.

During the weeks leading up to the riots, the *Daily Mirror* ran a series of articles by Keith Waterhouse, informing the predominantly White readers about the new wave of Black people who had settled in Britain. Under the headline: THE BOYS FROM JAMAICA, he wrote about the new wave of Jamaicans in Britain like this:

> ... People are human beings even though they come in different colours... the main reason for the riots is plain ignorance ... they are not heathens, they are not stealing homes and jobs ... (Sept.8, 1958).

The *Daily Mirror* was perceived to be taking a 'right on' approach in its editorial themes and contents.

Pear Connor told me:

> We were all involved in Notting Hill marches, the racist killing of Kelso Cochrane and the riots brought us all together. The writers and artists got involved.

After the Notting Hill disturbances, in which only Whites rioted (see Hall, 1991), the Government of the day under Macmillan began to talk of more stringent immigration control. Lord Hailsham, in a Cabinet paper, claimed that 'property has been bought up by coloured landlords, who have then made the position of White tenants intolerable, and entire streets have gone over to a coloured population.' He claimed that 'many immigrants are accustomed to living in squalid conditions and have no desire to improve their surroundings'.

The *West Indian Gazette* appeared and was to set the precedent for West Indian newspaper publishing in Britain in the 1950s. It challenged racism and the laws on immigration which were basically aimed at Black people; it offered an alternative and opposing voice; it promoted the Black cause. Though the intention was to create a popular tabloid, it did not concern itself with tittle-tattle as did the mainstream tabloids, but was a campaigning news organ which presented news with a serious political perspective. In its editorial themes and contents, it openly condemned the Immigration Bill and colonial actions such as the Portuguese interference, aided by South African troops, in Mozambique.

Claudia Jones was actively involved in the wider campaign for social justice and human rights and in the *West Indian Gazette* she supported political organisations who were sympathetic to the cause. Pearl Connor described how Claudia Jones kept in regular contact with people such as American civil right activists Paul Robeson and Martin Luther King. When Martin Luther King stopped off in London to collect the Nobel Peace Prize, Pearl Connor held a reception for him at her home, that was attended by Robeson, Jones and others working for change.

Between 1958 and 1961 a number of lobbying organisations sprang up. In 1958, Norman Manley, Chief Minister of Jamaica, flew to London to launch the Standing Conference of West Indian Organisations, later the West Indian Standing Conference. Claudia Jones joined with Frances Ezzrecco to found the Coloured People's Progressive Association and led a group of lobbyists from the organisation's offices to the Home Secretary to campaign on behalf of Black people living in Britain. The Indian Workers Association was formed, after Nehru visited London and apparently advised on setting up such a body for Indians in Britain. The Pakistani Workers' Association was established in 1961.

In 1962, the Commonwealth Immigration Bill was presented to Parliament. Lord Butler, Home Secretary, told the Cabinet that 'it would be desirable to seek to establish some form of control over the immigration of Black people.'

In August 1963, the prominent Black lobbying organisations, under the Conference of Afro-Asian Caribbean Organisations (CAACO) established in 1961, organised a march opposing the Immigration Act. In spite of wide condemnation, the Immigration Bill finally became Law under a Labour Government.

The *West Indian Gazette* articulated the implications of these political issues and supported the wider Pan-African issues. Its friends and allies included Bertrand Russell, Fenner Brockway and some of Claudia Jones's contemporaries such as Pearl Connor and the Canadian actress Isabell Lucas and *The Gazette's* sports editor, Theo Campbell, a former volunteer from Jamaica stationed with the Royal Air Force, in Lyneham, Wiltshire, who served in Transport Command between 1942 and 1947, provided an office base for the paper. Campbell had settled in South London in 1955 and established the first Black travel agency and a record shop in Brixton. He later became editor of *JOFFA* Magazine.

Claudia Jones edited the *West Indian Gazette* from 1958 to 1963. She divided her time

Claudia Jones

between working on the newspaper and travelling to the numerous speaking engagements to which she was invited. In 1962, for instance, she spent several months in the Soviet Union as a guest of the editors of a Soviet magazine, 'Soviet Women'. In 1964 she travelled to Japan to attended the World Conference against the Hydrogen Bomb and in 1964 she toured China.

A series of tragic events led Claudia Jones to move to Britain. Her mother died of overwork and poverty in the United States in 1927, less than three years after arriving there. Fired by a sense of injustice she joined the Communist Party in America in 1934, at the age of eighteen. In 1936, she was offered a place to study drama but chose instead to work with the *New York Daily Worker* (the American Communist Party newspaper). After years of poor health and overwork, Claudia Jones died an untimely death in her home in Hampstead, on 25th December 1964. She is buried in Highgate Cemetery, next to Karl Marx.

The *West Indian Gazette and Afro-Asian Caribbean News* — its full title — continued publishing until May, 1965. The final edition was published from 58 Lisburne Road in Hampstead.

After the *West Indian Gazette's* demise every new Black newspaper or magazine was to be a welcome entry to the Black media in Britain. Over the next decades, however, some 20 newspapers and magazines published by various activists and entrepreneurs have been unable to keep going. *Flamingo* for example, launched in December 1960, was produced from offices at 57 Charlton Street, London NW1. It featured a wide range of human interest stories and interviews on prominent Black people from both the classical and contemporary periods. The writers included Jan Carew and its editor, Edward Scobie. *Flamingo's* main objective was to demonstrate that Blacks do not have to be portrayed as boot polishers and street sweepers. It provided evidence that Black people had contributed in all walks of life. Robert Browning, for example, an acclaimed British poet of the 19th century, was the child of a Negro-White marriage. Others included Queen Charlotte Sophia, wife of George III; Beethoven, Haydn, Benjamin Disraeli, Alexander Dumas, Victor Hugo and Samuel Coleridge-Taylor.

One story featured Rudolph Dunbar, 'the brilliant Negro conductor' from British Guiana. He was the first 'Negro' to conduct the London Philharmonic Orchestra at the Royal Albert Hall, which he did during the War. Three years later he conducted the Berlin Philharmonic Orchestra at the Titiana Palace in Berlin. The critics wrote that, in an event of historic political proportions, he was the first non-German since the Nazi regime and the first Negro to conduct a Berlin Orchestra.

In its first issue *Flamingo* reported that:

> Chief Albert John Luthuli, President-General of the African National Congress in South Africa has been awarded the Nobel Peace Price... Luthuli was among the 156 who originally appeared (with Nelson Mandela) at the treason trial, but later allegations against him and sixty others were withdrawn... He shares the honour with Dag Hammarskjold and has been awarded the sum of £15,600.

Labour Peer and medical doctor, Lord Pitt and the former Prime Minister of Jamaica, Michael Manley featured in its pages, among other prominent Blacks but within a few years *Flamingo* was history.

Chapter 5

THE HEADY DAYS OF
THE 1970s

The rebellious 1960s heralded the Black cultural identity. Hair, clothes and posturing were redefined and the early '70s still basked in the afterglow. Radical and fashion-conscious Blacks alike adopted the afro hair-do and they donned African printed fabrics and rejected Western styles, culture and vocabulary. The slogan: 'Say it aloud, I'm Black and I'm proud' was imported from the United States, newly emerged from the Civil Rights movement. Names such as Martin Luther King, Angela Davis and Malcolm X became synonymous with the struggle. Blacks in America and Europe had found a new assertiveness and self-pride.

It was into this scenario that the *West Indian World* was launched by Aubrey Baynes, a St. Vincent-born graduate of business and economics from a North American university who had long been associated with the Black Press. Donald Hinds, head of history at a Southwark school and a former contributor to the *West Indian Gazette*, told me that for a time, Baynes had in the 1960s edited a magazine called *Magnet*. Baynes started the *West Indian World* with assistance of Antigua-born photographer, Caudley George; Guyana-born barrister, Rudy Narayan; South African-born journalist, Lionel Morrison and Jamaicans Tony Douglas and Rhoden Gordon. They started the newspaper with 'very little cash and a lot of good intentions', at a cover price of 5p. It began its publishing life at 340 Kilburn Lane, London, W9.

The first issue on 11th June, 1971 led with a story by Lord Campbell:

> In Britain's sugar colonies, sugar, it used to be said, was king. Most of them are now independent countries and plantations have become modern sugar industries. King sugar is often a political Aunt Sally... The sugar plantations by and large were founded by Europeans... founded on slave labour.
>
> The present British government... has gone out of its way to highlight Commonwealth sugar as a problem which must be solved... an interest which must be protected in the Common Market negotiations... I like to think that there is some sense of moral obligation and of debts unpaid.

A former correspondent reminisces that *The West Indian World* sought to set the political, social and media trends of the 1970s, and its news pages were full of controversial social issues concerning the Black communities. News stories featured poor housing conditions, lack of employment opportunities and social inequalities. The intention was to shame the establishment into taking notice of their situations:

> We received correspondence from key establishment figures such as Home Office Ministers.
>
> When Race Relations Units and Equal Opportunity initiatives emerged in local councils in some years, it was felt that the *West Indian World* helped the establishment to be made more aware of the various social conditions affecting Black people in Britain.

Within only six months the *West Indian World* fell into financial difficulties. Baynes left to go back to St Vincent and Arif Ali, who already owned the quarterly *West Indian Digest*, stepped in and took over the paper. In 1971 he bought out Baynes' shares, a risky thing to do considering that the paper relied on small black businesses as its main source of advertising revenue and even that was not guaranteed.

Tony Douglas told me:

> What you had was a newspaper which started with an idea from Aubrey Baynes and you had people like me who believed that here

Above: Harold Wilson touring Nottinghill after the 1974 Carnival riots with Tony Douglas.

Left: Douglas, the Campaigner

Below: Michael Manley, with the Jamaica High Commissioner, Arthur Wint and Douglas.

was a media that could counter-balance the negative things that were being said by the national media about Black people.

When the paper started we were never paid, but I didn't mind working for nothing at all because we believed in what we were doing. Quite a lot of English people were also supportive of the paper. We had Clayton Goodwin, who now writes for the *Jamaican Gleaner;* Zena Mason, a friend of Aubrey Baynes's, who had put up money as shareholder. It was quite a multiracial team. There was also Lionel Morrison, who taught me a great deal about journalism; Neil Kenlock, now Choice FM Director, who was our photographer. I stayed with the *West Indian World* for over ten years and was its editor for four years.

One of the major problems for the *West Indian World* was lack of advertisements, as Douglas explains:

There is no way in the 1970s that we would get advertising because we'd go to the local council and the companies and they'd say Black people don't have any money, they don't spend any money and our major task was to prove to them that Black people have got an income, that they've got a market, that they do spend money, they do buy cars; so that was our difficulty.

Working against such obstacles, and with their printers still needing payment for work, they were unable to pay their bills. They skipped from one printer to another to keep the paper going. With Arif Ali, their new publisher, they moved from Kilburn to Mathias Road in Stoke Newington. Again the debts kept on rising.

Tony Douglas was not reticent about the ups and downs of the former flagship Black newspaper. He admits:

When Arif took over the paper he had the goodwill of a Black publication and worked very hard. He also brought in his wife and family and they worked towards keeping the paper going. But having said that, Arif is a very egotistical person and that's one of the reasons he worked extremely hard to keep the paper going.

At the same time we were working seven days a week too, but we had no money in our pockets. We were on the motorway going to whichever printers we could get to keep the paper going.

You had a situation where Arif started approaching various Caribbean governments regarding various projects for the newspaper, various supplements, which some of them who were very egotistical themselves, agreed to.

Arif started believing that he was a head of state himself and he decided to move to Barbados — he took his whole family and he was hob-nobbing with the Prime Minister, Errol Barrow. He would fly back to London whenever he felt like it and meanwhile back at base, we were struggling and not knowing where the next printers' bill was coming from. While Arif was putting his feet up in Barbados, there were times when I had only £10 a week to take home to my family. Although he had fifty-one percent shares in the paper we called a meeting in his absence and decided: this can't go on, we've got to get rid of Arif.

In his usual presidential style, Arif telephoned the office to say: he's flying in and he wants to be picked up at the airport. Neil Kenlock intended to use the company car to pick them up and I said to him, no way, you take the van and you take up Arif and his family — if they don't want to travel in the van that's their business. Neil picked up Arif, dropped his family home and when he arrived in the office no one wanted to say anything because everyone behaved as if they were frightened of him. We went into what was then his office and I said to him, look, Arif, your time is up, we've had enough. He asked the rest of the staff what they thought and everyone kept quiet. He took the silence to mean a vote of no confidence and he eventually cleared his desk and left.

So in effect, Tony Douglas was responsible for ousting Arif from the *West Indian World*. From then on they tried to work as a co-operative. One of the people, apart from Zena Morrison, who bailed the paper out was a Jamaican property developer called Joe Whitter. He put up several of his properties as security for a bank loan and backed the *West Indian*

World for over five years. Today a multi-millionaire and living in Jamaica, back then he was nicknamed 'Slidey' Joe Whitter and was hounded by the national media and various authorities. While living in Forest Hill, South-East London, he bought a row of properties from a local organisation and rented them out — and the national tabloids branded him a 'SLUM LANDLORD.'

Tony Douglas, Caudley George and several others moved with the *West Indian World* to 36 West Green Road in 1981. The paper was to change ownership again, this time under the management of Caudley George. He negotiated a deal with the others by which he out-manoeuvred them and gained control of the paper. Some found the deal unacceptable and ultimately Caudley George, Tony Douglas and other interested parties settled the matter in the High Court. The judge ruled in Caudley George's favour and Tony Douglas was ousted. I remarked on the irony that Tony Douglas suffered the same fate as Arif Ali a few years earlier. It was less messy though: Arif unceremoniously moved out without resorting to Court action.

'Slidey' Joe Whitter at the head of the table Credit: Neil Kenlock

Douglas admits:

> It was the most depressing time of my life when I had to move out,
> I actually cried. I was committed to that newspaper one hundred
> percent and to see Caudley George, a self-confessed Pentecostal
> Christian, someone whom we trusted, bamboozle us like that was
> heart-breaking.

Mike Phillips, already a freelance columnist on the paper and an
experienced freelance journalist in mainstream press and broadcasting,
was appointed editor of *West Indian World*. In spite of the paper's record
of financial unreliability, it has over the years attracted experienced
journalists, already working freelance in the mainstream, who were
ready to make the sacrifices. Mike Phillips (brother of television
executive Trevor) edited the paper from 1981 to 1983. He told me that
he had 'worked for all the national Fleet Street newspapers apart from
the *Sun*'. He had also worked as a freelance in broadcasting and
presented a BBC World Service radio series, 'Caribbean Magazine',
previously presented by Trevor McDonald.

Phillips eventually left to take up a post as a senior lecturer in journalism
at the University of Westminster, a job which he held from 1983 to 1993,
since when he has become an author and scriptwriter. He takes pride in
the fact that some of the people he has taught at the University include
the present BBC Programme Controller, Michael Jackson, BBC
'Clothes Show' presenter, Brenda Emmanus and X-Press Publisher,
Steve Pope.

The staff of *West Indian World* worked under difficult conditions. More
often than not, their miserly journalism fees were paid in cheques which
bounced, and holiday pay and sick pay was virtually non-existent. There
was a great deal of editorial commitment on the part of the journalists
in spite of financial problems. There was also a loyal readership from
the mainly West Indian readers who knew and trusted the paper to report
on issues which affected them. But the newspaper suffered from
insufficient financial backing and had far too few advertisements to
make it economically viable.

From the start the *West Indian World's* financial problems were severe. Yet throughout the 1970s, there was very little competition from other West Indian publishers, the only real threat coming from the short-lived *Caribbean Weekly Post* in the mid-1970s. Reality Publishing, parent company of the *West Indian World,* started a magazine, *Focus,* but this lasted only a few months. With the multiple problems of a virtually non-existent public sector or corporate advertisements, and a diminishing circulation in the face of stiff competition from two new contenders in the early 1980s, the *Caribbean Times* and the *Voice*, meant that the newspaper's days were numbered.

By 1985 the *West Indian World* folded, under Caudley George's management. The last editor was Trinidad-born journalist, Alfred Tang Chow. He told me that he was offered a weekly wage of £60 and worked without pay on the ailing newspaper for a year 'because he had an ego to feed'. He has, he said spent over 20 years in the industry. He was approached for advice on the *West Indian World* by Russell Pierre, a Grenadian, whom he described as 'someone who has tinkered with publishing', with Caudley George. Chow was very critical of some of the publishing as 'very amateurish'.

Goodwill alone was not enough to save the paper. The National Union of Journalists was brought in to help sort out the journalists' grievances. Attempts were made to produce other newspapers soon afterwards, using some of the *West Indian World* staff, but these papers were blacklisted by the NUJ and the publishers' plans frustrated. In its fourteen years, the *West Indian World* earned its place in the history of the Black media in Britain as the longest running post-war West Indian-owned newspaper.

Tony Douglas bought the *West Indian World* title from the liquidators for £1000, and he has the last word:

> I have my heart in the *West Indian World*. It was the first and I vow it won't be the last of it.

Chapter 6

IN PURSUIT OF EQUALITY

Out of the immigration pattern of the 1950s and 1960s emerged the second generation of Blacks who grew up in the UK, and then a third and fourth generation of British-born Blacks. Today, they share similar educational and cultural experiences and aspirations to their White counterparts. They have much the same ideals and expect the same opportunities but most feel that they have been denied this right. Yet they have an interest in what is in effect their society in general and are a part of it.

They expect the same opportunities but the only thing that has dramatically changed, both in society in general and in the media in particular, is a greater awareness, brought about partly by campaigning and partly by the increased Black population and economic growth. Many are optimistic, however, that real change will come. For one thing, the media have been made aware of their obligations. Broadcasting standards, for example, are governed by codes of conduct and there are statutory obligations regarding equality in the job market and this will, in the medium to long term, have an impact on the print media.

As long as Black people feel left out of the mainstream and have no mainstream representative voice they obviously have to speak for themselves. And one of the most effective ways of doing this is through newspaper, radio or television. If the Black community support Black media organs in significant numbers, their success will pose a threat to the wider media, which will in turn help to force change. But then again,

Black newspaper and magazine publishers have to rise to the challenge of improving their standards and managing their finances.

Today the heart of Black progressiveness is not only in the Pan-African organisation. Westernised Blacks, through campaigning groups and Black news organs and journals, are calling for equal opportunities for Africans and the descendants of Africans in the media and the wider society. In the early 1980s various campaigning media organisations were set up to challenge the mainstream on the issue of equal opportunities in the media. A dearth of significant Black representation led to the launch of campaigning groups such as the Black Media Workers Association (BMWA) in 1981, and the Black Research Workers Network. Black professionals from African, Asian and Caribbean backgrounds, such as Perminder Vir, Mike Phillips and Diane Abbott, now a Labour MP, came together with academics such as Safder Alladina.

Safder Alladina told me:

> We were people who met socially from time to time and who gradually became aware that the problems that were faced by the Black media workers were of common expression. Feelings of isolation, frustration and alienation were felt in such a way as to become a focal rallying point for something more than a supportive solidarity.

The BMWA was formally launched in February 1981 at a meeting of over 150 people from various backgrounds. It focused on two major concerns: the concerns of the media profession, and of the Black community in society. The BMWA approached the National Union of Journalists (NUJ), who supported their aim to tackle the problem of Black representation. The NUJ in turn laid down basic guidelines whereby both media coverage and media employment would fully reflect the reality of Britain's multiracial society.

An NUJ-backed Race Relations Working Party was addressing similar issues. The political activist and journalist, Marc Wadsworth acknowledges that the Commission for Racial Equality and the trade unions lobbied for change in employment practices in the workplace.

In some media organisations, little has changed since but others are gradually moving towards change.

The *Guardian*, which is perceived to be a relatively liberal paper, currently employs four Black journalists and two sub-editors. Angella Johnson is one of the four writers:

> On the scale of one to three in terms of seniority all of the Black journalists on the paper are at scale three. There are no women or Blacks at the top but at scale two there are three women.

> The *Guardian* is a liberal newspaper and it prides itself on highlighting Black issues in a positive way; more so than any other paper except maybe the *Observer* and the *Independent.* But we have a long way to go before they appoint women in very senior positions. There are two or three women at the middle rank and lots of us women down at scale three.

> Blacks haven't worked on the *Guardian* as long as women have and it's taken women a long time to be called. But I think as people come in with the experience and the educational background, bright Black people will eventually get on... I hope!

The press have been slow in rising to the challenge but broadcasters are now rising to it and may show the way forward. The Broadcasting Act contains a clause specifying that large broadcasting companies are obliged to make some commitment to equal opportunities in hiring staff. Companies such as the celestial Sky Television have a long way to go but some of the terrestrials, in particular the BBC, have been making inroads, although not without difficulties. But despite the few Black faces now seen on television there are only almost no non-White executives. Samir Shah at the BBC is head of news and current affairs. Trevor Phillips was head of current affairs at London Weekend Television but has recently resigned to concentrate on making programmes and Farrukh Dhondy at Channel Four is a Commissioning Editor dealing exclusively with minority programming.

One independent television producer and former BBC producer who was once the editor of *Voice* newspaper, expressed his concern that many

Black journalists who went into the BBC, mainly, from black newspapers in the 1980s have 'hit the glass ceiling' and he believes those who moved to the national press have fared rather better:

> Blacks who went from say the *Voice* newspaper to the BBC were interested in career development as well as radical change but the BBC is a conservative media machine and some of those who opted for both were fighting on two fronts.

Another, Colin Prescod, said that he was appointed producer in the BBC's Afro-Caribbean Unit after Vashtiana Belfon resigned but that he too left. Apparently they decided to merge the unit with another and this affected his position. When he was asked if he would like another job within the Corporation he declined because he was critical of the way staff were treated. He received four months pay and quit.

Nevertheless, the BBC hopes to employ some eight percent Black journalists by the year 2000, which one hopes will begin to make a difference. In the meantime, there is still the question of Blacks in media employment and in senior positions in both broadcasting and the mainstream press. Of some 63 editors in the mainstream quality press, none are Black, nor are any of the 75 or so editors on the national tabloids. Out of a total of some 4,000 journalists there are about 20 Black journalists in the mainstream press.

Black media working parties and, to a certain extent, liberal Whites have played a leading role in the improvement of conditions for Blacks in the media and continue to lead the way in improving conditions for Black journalists and potential journalists. For instance, the University of Westminster provides journalism training courses for unemployed Asians and African-Caribbeans. Some of these trainees might go on to higher education in journalism at other institutes such as the London College of Printing or elsewhere in London and the regions or be offered employment in the media.

Today there are also journalism courses and further education colleges which people like the long-established Black journalist, Syd Burke, presenter of the former London Broadcasting Company (LBC) series, 'Rice 'n' Peas'; and the South African-born journalist and NUJ executive, Lionel Morrison have helped to set up at Vauxhall College and Brixton College. Community media centres are dotted around the country, backed jointly by local authorities and the Arts Council. These are mainly in inner city areas, such as the Kirklees Media Centre in Huddersfield, centres in inner-London Deptford, Hackney and Brixton — and in other multiracial conurbations. Some media studies groups in schools and further education colleges such as Hammersmith and West London College have mentoring schemes. So there is evidence of some positive results gained from campaigning for change: getting training courses off the ground, improving employment conditions and developing a representative media image in general from grass roots level to mainstream.

At the forefront of Black media awareness campaigns for racial equality, equitable representation in employment and reportage of stories about the Black communities in Britain today, are the National Union of Journalists and the Commission For Racial Equality. Which is just as well because a number of the independent Black groups which were actively campaigning for a better media environment for Black people in the 1980s have dissolved. An organisation called the Black Journalists' Association was founded in 1989 by former editor of the *Asian Herald* Iqbal Wahhab, *Financial Times* reporter Joel Kibazo and BBC producer David Upshall but it exists largely as a networking and support group for fellow journalists.

In 1992, the CRE launched the first Race In The Media Awards, a national award to acknowledge journalists and broadcasters — Black and White alike — who have made significant contributions in their work to creating better understanding of racial and social issues. Backed by trade unions, it had a board of executives which included broadcaster Trevor Phillips, actors Floella Benjamin and the late Norman Beaton, former actress and university lecturer Lola Young and sports personality Garth Crooks. Several hundred national newspaper journalists and broadcasters, as well as journalists from the provincial and ethnic press and community radio were nominated for the first RIMA and nearly fifty were short-listed in seven categories.

The national newspaper category for 1992 was won by Black journalist Hugh Muir, formerly of the *Mail on Sunday,* and by then at the *Daily Telegraph.* Black journalists who work on the national dailies have to work for the ethos of that market so Hugh Muir has doubly broken down barriers. Muir won his award for his series of reports on the racism experienced by Black soldiers in the armed forces, under the following headings: 'Hatred that forced a soldier to run away', 'Mother joins up for battle', 'Race case soldier in suicide attempt', 'Charles does not care, says black soldier', 'Probe over soldiers in race abuse ordeal', 'Another Black squaddie to leave', 'Army acts on racists', and 'Stars and Strife in the 51st State'.

Hugh Muir receiving his award
Credit: CRE

The CRE's Chief Executive and co-founder of the Award, Herman Ouseley is only too aware that:

> Writers, performers and journalists are at the sharp end in helping to bring about change. The Race in the Media Award is a good initiative but by itself will not bring about the transformation we all want to see. Co-operation is important in bringing about change, promoting a greater awareness and learning from each other on matters of race.

According to the CRE's press officer, Chris Myant, the *Sun's* deputy editor told him that the add-on reader they are hunting is more likely to be Black than White and that their Black readership outstrips the *Voice* readership throughout Britain. The *Sun* is also addressing race, he says:

> We did a survey and put two guys in a flash car — one Black guy and one White — and the young Black guy got stopped by the police but the White guy didn't.

Chris Myant does not believe that pressure groups alone will force change in the mainstream either, but he does support the argument that the increased Black spending power will be a major factor. He added:

> Not so long ago Piers Morgan who is now editor on the *News of the World,* who previously wrote a column in the *Sun,* ran stories about Black stars in the media. The *Sun* also ran stories denouncing racism in music and racism in sport.

When Myant was asked whether the stories pertaining to music and sport could be considered to be a supple form of media stereotyping, he agreed that the *Sun's* ploy is much more sophisticated but said that they appeal to diverse and contradictory audiences. He cited Richard Littlejohn and Brian Hayes as examples of provocateurs whose journalistic approach increases readership and audience ratings.

Chris Myant believes that the *News of the World* is also tackling the race issue. But he raised the point that certain tabloids do play their race cards, particularly on immigration, at certain times — shortly before local and general elections, for instance. He is optimistic that things will get better, however and even gave an example of improved race reporting by the *News of the World* in a double page spread on racial violence, adding that 'the story was angry, sharp and very critical.' Nevertheless, these are just the occasional pieces. He did however express his concern that the *Daily Star* targets a White prejudiced readership and is not interested in taking up a marketing approach that would appeal to a more racially diverse readership.

Herman Ouseley
Credit: Terry Austin-Smith

When the European Union is in full swing, the Black media debate will obviously move to another dimension and already we are beginning to see this happening. The issue of equitable media representation now extends beyond Britain's boundaries to EU countries such as France, the Netherlands and Germany, where significant concentrations of Africans and descendants of Africa are born and have established roots.

Herman Ouseley is confident that there is a fair amount of collaboration with Europe and said that foundations were established in 1992, almost simultaneously with the CRE's Race In the Media Foundation. In Holland for example, the European Migrant Media Prize (EMMP), operating under the auspices of the Council of Europe and the European Broadcasting Union (EBU) in Geneva, was founded by Anti-Discriminatie Overleg in the Netherlands, the CRE in London and representation from Brussels, Paris and Cologne. Another Europe-wide organisation, the Standing Conference for Race Equality in Europe (SCORE), which is chaired by Bernie Grant, MP, challenges racist structures that deny fair treatment to Blacks. But as this book goes to press there are reports of internal wranglings within SCORE.

Controversy of this kind makes a mockery of the campaigning groups, which on one hand advocate equality and harmonisation and on the other hand are themselves embroiled in disharmony.

George Ruddock

Chapter Seven

THE ENTREPRENEURIAL AGE

By the mid-1980s, a large number of the African-Caribbean media organisations began moving to the heart of Brixton, South London. There one will find the *Weekly Gleaner* which is read mainly by Jamaican migrant groups, *The Voice, Artrage* and Choice FM. The *Gleaner's* current editor is George Ruddock, brought over from Jamaica to fill the post. He explains that the British edition is intended for Jamaicans living in Britain in the 20 to 60 age group and that 'It is a 'middle-of-the-road, non-political family newspaper'. Seventy percent of the *Gleaner's* editorial contents focuses on news events in Jamaica and thirty percent on regional news events about Jamaicans living in Britain, with a Black perspective.

He also pointed out that although they have freelancers, the regional news from around Britain is sometimes submitted by the local communities. But Robert Govender argues that the British edition of *The Gleaner* is a let-down:

> Two of the oldest established Black newspapers in Britain today are the *Jamaican Gleaner* and *West Africa* but the *Gleaner* has failed to make an impact on the wider society.

The *Gleaner* was founded in Jamaica in 1834, in the same year slavery was abolished. Govender was formerly editor of a free distribution magazine, *Nine-To-Five* and is the author of several books on politics, including *The Martyrdom of Patrice Lumumba* and *Nicolae Ceausescu*

And The Romanian Road To Socialism. Due to unforeseen circumstances, Robert Govender's latter book did not end up a best-seller, after the Romanian government under Ceausescu was toppled.

The *Gleaner* moved to Brixton, South London, from prestigious offices based at the International Press Centre, Shoe Lane, off Fleet Street — once the heartland of the newspaper industry. It was published by Kent Messenger Group. Ruddock pointed out that:

> Kent Messenger Group was themselves having problems of industrial unrest and because of such strikes we had to move because of the unreliability of the printers at the time. So once we moved from Kent Messenger Group the facilities at the International Press Centre which was owned by the Group went with it.

> The idea of moving to Brixton was an ideal opportunity to come into the heart of the Black community.

George Ruddock has been its managing editor since its move to Brixton. And the *Gleaner* has been taken down-market editorially, in a bid for a more popular tabloid appeal. Its loyal readership remains mainly West Indians, particularly Jamaicans, interested in news from 'back home'. In spite of the Jamaica-based *Daily Gleaner's* formidable history, spanning over one hundred and fifty years, making it the oldest Black newspaper in existence today, the British edition is not without its critics. They argue that it lacks the editorial direction and news construction associated with most of today's respected newspapers.

Has 'the *Times* of the Caribbean' failed to move with the times? Indeed some of the articles which appear in the British edition are not recent news but, instead, extracts or rewrites from the previous weeks' *Daily Gleaner* in Jamaica. Would it not be more efficient to have the reports transmitted by a news agency, thus eliminating the problem of out-of-date stories and ensuring better value for money?

In Jamaica the *Gleaner* is a broadsheet newspaper still supporting the privileged elite, whilst the tabloid *Daily Star* supports working class idealism. The British edition of the *Gleaner* has had to shed much of its conservative image and adopt a more popular style of reporting to suit the wider social grouping of the Black British readership. But critics argue that it seems to have maintained a type of colonial mentality in its approach to news reporting and has hardly diverged editorially from the old style. Headlines such as NEEDY CITIZENS WAITING FOR SUPPLIES (22.5.1990) have appeared on its pages.

Many observers had began to predict that the paper to watch was the *Voice*. Born out of Vee Tee Ay Publishing, it later changed its company name to Voice Communications Group. Some say that it was the *West Indian World* that paved the way for the *Voice's* success because by the time the *Voice* appeared on the scene in 1982 Black social awareness had gained momentum.

The *Caribbean Times* appointed a young editor, Mike Massive, in the mid-1980s, to follow Dan Harriet, also a young Black Briton. Many were expecting a radical change in the way the paper was presented but it did not happen.

This was a time when Thatcherism was at its height with all emphasis on free enterprise, economic progress and capital gain. It was an era when the Black Upwardly Mobile Professionals (BUPPIES) and Young Urban Professionals (YUPPIES) were emerging; a time when media advertising was at a peak.

The founder and owner of Hansib Publishing Company, Arif Ali controlled the largest number of newspaper and periodical titles in Black publishing in Britain, regularly producing approximately five newspapers and periodicals in addition to books. At one time he owned the *West Indian Digest*, *African Times*, *Asian Times*, *Caribbean Times* and *Asian Digest*.

Hansib Publishing company has a history of media acquisitions. Ali acquired *Root* in 1987 from its founding publishers, Patrick Berry and Neil Kenlock. *Root* started life in prestigious

Patrick Berry

premises in Duke Street in the heart of Mayfair. After they sold it, Kenlock and Berry concentrated their efforts on developing their media plans for the broadcasting licence, acquired in 1990, and both are now directors of *Choice FM,* the South London and Birmingham based Black music station.

Massive claims that the *Caribbean Times,* expresses the particular perspective of a campaigning newspaper that addresses political issues. He told me that: '25,000 copies of *The Caribbean Times* are distributed nationally each week'. This equates to a readership then in the region of 100,000 — which is pitiful when you consider the number of African-Caribbeans who read the *Sun.*

Clockwise from left: Arif Ali with Trevor MacDonald, Nelson Mandela and Sonny Ramphal.
Credit: Caribbean Times

At the height of the entrepreneurial 1980s there were some 70 staff members working at Hansib Publishing; today there are twelve. Their titles have been shrinking too: '*Root Magazine, The West Indian Digest* and *African Times* are now on hold but what's left are *The Asian Times* and *The Caribbean Times*,' says Mike Massive.

Hansib also has an eclectic book publishing operation: Dr David Dabydeen's epic prize-winning poem, *Coolie Odyssey*, Dr Aaron Haynes's *State of Black Britain*, Ashton Gibson and Dame Jocelyn Barrow's *The Unequal Struggle*, Sir Shridath Ramphal's *Inseparable Humanity* and the Prime Minister of Guyana, Cheddi Jagan's *Forbidden Freedom* indicate the distinction and diversity of the authors.

Colleague Robert Govender sees him as the modern Black pioneer in magazine and newspaper publishing, a title he has earned for over twenty years. He believes that had Ali been born white, he would by now be on the same financial footing as Rupert Murdoch.

Take the situation with the *West Indian World*. When it fell into financial difficulties in 1971 after only six months, Arif Ali took it over even though he had already acquired the *West Indian Digest,* an international current affairs magazine which was already doing well. This appeared pretty risky considering that *WIW* relied solely on small Black· businesses for revenue from advertising and even that source of revenue was not always guaranteed.

The *Voice* on the other hand, encapsulated the mood of young Black Britons. In January 1981, thirteen young Black people were burned to death at a party in New Cross. The handling by the authorities and the media of the New Cross fire precipitated a protest march by 10,000 people, White as well as Black, and the tabloids presented it under headlines such as BLACK MOB RAMPAGE. The frustration and anger that had erupted into riots in British cities was in urgent need of a voice.

By identifying and serving this misrepresented sector of society, the *Voice* made an historic break from the past. According to former editor, Onyekachi Wambu, 'all the other papers had one foot here and one foot there'. But the *Voice*, calling itself the voice of Black Britain, was saying: it does not matter if your ethnic background is Aborigine or Zulu

— if it's an issue which affects Black Britons, let's report it. The other newspapers had never quite departed from the image of being papers for mainly first generation Black settlers from a specific part of the world.

Wambu — himself born in Nigeria — added:

> The difference is that the *Voice* was being edited by the ones who had been brought up in Britain and this injected a new dimension into Black news reporting in Britain.

Val McCalla, a Jamaican-born accountant founded the *Voice* with an initial team which included Grenada-born Alex Pascall, formerly a BBC radio broadcaster on the weekly 'Black Londoners', Viv Broughton, Tony Brown and Robert Govender. The publishing company received backing from Barclays Bank and from the Labour Party-led Greater London Council (GLC). The editorial offices were above a video store in Mare Street, Hackney, one of the poorest boroughs in London. The Pascall and McCalla liaison ended acrimoniously soon after the newspaper was founded.

Alex Pascall with Angela Davis

Robert Govender's short-lived association as the first editor on the *Voice* came to an abrupt end. He talked about his summary dismissal: 'I was sacked. The publisher over-ruled my editorial decision over a front page story and I objected to his decision'. The national press carried the story of the sacking.

Alex Pascall's and Robert Govender's departure from the paper was followed by a new breed of younger journa-lists and additional staff. Flip Fraser, who was born in Jamaica but grew up in Britain, was appointed editor after Govender. Meanwhile, Viv Broughton, a White member of the management committee who had been with

Onyekachi Wambu

the paper from the start had, together with a team of marketing and promotions enthusiasts, developed a series of sharp marketing strategies to promote the paper and increase its readership and sales. The editorial team was equally committed to the newspaper's success. But the *Voice* suffered immense cash flow problems at the early stages and very often the staff's salaries went unpaid for days. Nevertheless, they stayed on, working long hours because they were committed to a paper which offered them exciting opportunities.

Onyekachi Wambu commented on those early days:

> I'm not going to get into the argument over whether anyone was exploited or not, Val McCalla gave us the opportunity to do some exciting things. At the age of 24, Val gave me the opportunity when

no one else was prepared to give me the opportunity. He said, 'here you are, you are 24 you are the assistant editor'. He did not interfere and I'll always be grateful for that.

I'm not going to say, OK, when we first started he was paying me £50 a week so therefore I was exploited. We were told very clearly that the paper couldn't pay any more at that time (1984). But we were committed to journalism and he offered us the opportunity when others didn't.

Onye later became editor of the *Voice*, where he stayed for four years.

Both Broughton and McCalla had worked on *East End News* so they were not entirely strangers to the world of publishing. Twelve years later the Broughton-McCalla liaison still works. Broughton is now Marketing Director of Voice Communications Limited and another pioneering board member is its Production Director, Tony Brown who ran the newspapers' design department. Trinidad-born Dame Jocelyn Barrow, former governor of the BBC, is among the non-executive board members.

Voice Communications Group diversified into magazine publishing, producing *Chic, Black Beat International* and *Pride Magazine,* and into music management, signing up such artists as Mica Paris and Lavine Hudson.

McCalla's company started off with a staff of twelve. By 1989 it had two additional titles and the workforce had increased to fifty. Today it is one of the biggest African-Caribbean companies in Britain.

The *Voice* has gone through four editorial stages since it started in 1982, coinciding with its steady succession of editors. First there was Govender, who was very much concerned with the South African issue as well as the wider global interest.

Then came the team of Flip Fraser as editor, and Sharon Ali and Asif Zubairy as assistant editor and features editor respectively. They produced a very populist and campaigning paper that developed out of the Colin Roach saga: 'Colin Roach, a young Black man was supposed to have gone into Stoke Newington Police Station and shot himself.'

The locals refused to believe it. The *Voice* followed that story to the bitter end and young East End Blacks and inner city youth became regular *Voice* readers because of its concern about what was happening in their community.

Flip Fraser had also turned a spotlight on Black music, which many believe to be exploited by the mainstream. Fraser helped to launch the short-lived title, *Black Beat International* in the early 1980s, the first Black glossy music monthly magazine in Britain to be owned and controlled by Black publishers. It focused on African, Caribbean and Black American music and proved very popular with the 18-35 age group. But the magazine came to an abrupt end after several issues because it was not supported by the music industry despite all they have gained from Black musical talent throughout history. Flip Fraser left soon after and has since launched a popular touring musical stage extravaganza, 'Black Heroes in the Hall of Fame' which toured Britain, America and the Caribbean.

At one time, a strict pecking order was perceived to operate at the *Voice,* so that the next in line would automatically get promoted to editor. After Flip's departure, it was the turn of the assistant editor, Anglo-Trinidadian Sharon Ali to become editor. She later moved into broadcasting when offered a job as researcher at London Weekend Television and then on to BBC television to work as producer on Youth Programmes headed by Janet Street-Porter. The Pakistani-born Asif also went to work for London Weekend Television.

The next stage came towards the end of the mid-1980, with Kolton Lee as editor and Onyekachi Wambu as assistant editor. By then the company had moved to larger offices in Bow Road, East London. The paper was taken up-market at the height of the enterprise culture. The stories included features on Buppies, a 1980s phenomenon born out of Thatcher's Britain. An article in October 1987 read:

> ... left school at fourteen with no qualifications... 27 year old... annual turn over £500,000... house in St John's Wood, Hampstead and Marbella... fleet of cars including Porche with personalised number plates.'

In all, the feature focused on five people, all under 30 years old. It continued under the sub-heading '£35,000 a year and a BMW but no time for romance'...

> ... 28 years old...sales manager for publishers Readers Digest.... owns a £100,000 flat overlooking Wimbledon Tennis Club... weekend yachting trips...skiing *holidays in Gastaad,* Switzerland and Christmas touring the Caribbean.

Wambu explained:

> We continued in that populist mode but what we also did was to say, OK, most people who read this paper read the tabloids and there's no point offering them the *Guardian.*

> But within our community, you also have your *Guardian* readers. So you would lead with that populist tabloid style but try and have an editorial mix. So that in the features pages you can take the readers forward and have more substantive issues. At the time we looked at a whole range of stuff:

> There were features on the issue of Black achievement in schools and there was, for instance, a fifteen-page pull-out-supplement where we would introduce a big educational feature where we would look at Black education in Britain from 1945 to the present day. We would look at why Black children under-achieved in schools and what the educational establishment had done.

> There were features around the question of what was Reagan's foreign policy during the Grenada invasion but we did not actually go back to the Govender stage — the global feature was just one element. At home we said, look, there were things around the history of the riots we needed to understand.

> So the newspaper in a way becomes almost schizophrenic, but you need to do that with a certain kind of skill so you don't drive away the core audience. And in a sense you subtly change the habit of the core audience so that they have higher expectations.

Voice editor Kolton Lee left to take up a job as news editor on the *News on Sunday,* an ill-fated national tabloid, intended to be the people's newspaper, with particular appeal to a readership who would normally vote Labour. *News on Sunday* was financed by Trade Unions, left wing local authorities and celebrities who were interested in seeing a tabloid paper that had a left wing slant. At the time the idea was that the problem with tabloids in this country was that they present nothing but scandal and the broadsheets are inaccessible. The paper was meant to fill the gap. 'The paper came at a particular time when Thatcher was moving further and further to the right and Labour was tearing itself to pieces,' Kolton Lee comments. Within weeks it fell into difficulties and finally went into liquidation and the receivers were brought in. Kolton Lee explains:

> At that point the multi-millionaire Owen Oyston stepped in to back the paper. He cut staff, sold equipment and cut corners basically. I was demoted from being news editor. But from my point of view *News on Sunday* did not have enough money when it was launched. That's why the paper went into difficulties so soon after its launch. There was also a situation where Keith Sutton and John Pilger disagreed and one of them said it's either him or me. Pilger lost the battle, left, and Sutton took charge. But Sutton was not up to the job.

> I was the first Black journalist to be made an editor on a national newspaper — this was in 1987. I was one of three Black journalists working on the paper; the others were Belkis Begami and Barinder Kalsi. I tried to get other Black people in. I tried to get Egon Cossou, Onye Wambu and Tony Sewell in.

> I don't think Britain is ready to take on board the fact that this is a multiracial society and that you can have senior Black journalists whose agenda goes beyond the Black community.

Chapter 8

MODERN TIMES

Eight years down the line, most of Kolton Lee's generation of Black journalists who came through the *Voice* and moved into mainstream, have 'hit the glass ceiling'. Kolton Lee argues:

> Unlike your White counterparts who are of similar age and similar education and got in the media at the same time; eight years on, most of those journalists are either in senior positions in broadcasting or they are in senior positions on national newspapers.

> Here we are in 1994, a lot of the Black journalists who are of the same education and experience, are not doing nearly as well and if you are into conspiracy theories then just look around, because they are all out there, but they are not in the same level of seniority.

A year after Kolton Lee left the *Voice,* the company moved to Brixton. The succession of editors after Lee include Onye Wambu, Steve Pope and Winsome Cornish. During the Kolton Lee–Onye Wambu period, the paper tried to maintain its up-market appeal. But Steve Pope got acclaim for taking the paper down-market and broadening its news-as-entertainment-value. He located it at the heart of a populist market. Not necessarily populist in the sense of campaigning but in the sense of the *Sun* genre of sex, violence and sensationalism. As a result, sales and readership increased. Stories and features covered modelling and street scene tabloid titillation. Steve Pope outraged some readers with certain of the more controversial stories during his time as editor, to the extent that the paper issued an explanation to its readers. His reign as editor came to an end in 1991.

Val McCalla appointed the former *Chic* editor Winsome Cornish to edit the *Voice* and soon afterwards a staff reporter left to set up a weekly newspaper, *Black Briton*. There was much speculation over whether Pope left of his own accord or was forced out. Angella Johnson commented in The *Guardian*:

> Cornish replaces Steve Pope, leaving the paper under a cloud after six years. This follows a row over stories last October which were critical of footballer Justin Fashanu, who had declared his homosexuality in a national newspaper. Gay pressure groups accused the *Voice* of promoting homophobia and lobbied local councils, which in turn threatened to pull their large-scale advertising from the paper. *Voice's* management published an apology, but the incident exposed the paper's vulnerability.

However a publicity photograph which appeared in the February 1991 issue of the *Voice* showed Winsome Cornish and Steve Pope, smiling for the cameras, under the headline, NEW CAPTAIN FOR BRITAIN'S BEST and informing readers that after seven years at the *Voice*, Pope was looking for a new and diverse challenge. He was quoted as saying:

> I've had a fantastic time working at *The Voice* during a period of great change for the Black community, but I think now is the time to try something different. I have many unfulfilled ambitions.

Since then, Steve Pope has set up X-Press Publishing, specialising in sensationalist paperback novels.

Winsome Cornish

Public sector job advertisements have played a major part in keeping the *Voice* economically buoyant throughout much of its publishing life to date, although a number of commercial advertisements come from the American Black hair and cosmetics industry and more recently, corporate advertising. A separate bumper advertisement pull-out supplement was published each week for a time, often amounting to more than 40 pages.

A sixteen-page full colour supplement, *Now,* focused on arts and entertainment and there was also a free quarterly forty page general interest colour magazine supplement, *VS (Voice Supplement)*. *VS* and *Now* both carried numerous pages of colour advertisements, mainly from African-Caribbean and African-American entertainment and cosmetics industries. *AM/PM 24 Hours* has recently replaced *Now* and *VS*.

VS began in the mid-1980s, when the term Buppies was bandied about in reference to young Black professionals who earned good money and lived life in the fast lane. *Voice Supplement* had a trendy image which appealed to young Black professionals and aspiring groups at the time. The colour quarterly was distributed free with the *Voice* Newspaper and ran until the early 1990s. According to Mike Massive, editor of the *Caribbean Times*: '*VS* was much closer to what the market demands.'

However, with the late 1980s came a period of economic austerity and this affected both public and private sector organisations, with the result that advertisements became far less numerous. Since June 1994, however, full-page and double-page corporate advertisements from commercial organisations such as banks, building societies and car manufacturers have started to appear, although most of the advertisements still come from the public sector.

A recent analysis of the editorial contents of the *Voice* reveal fourteen pages focusing on local news, two on sport, a children's page, a religious page and two pages on international news. According to Steve Pope, a large proportion of readers are local government employees. But there is also a multiracial readership. It appeals to a greater extent to West Indians and Africans and to a lesser extent to Whites and Asians. Many people subscribe to it because it carries so many local government job advertisements. Its ABC rating is 50,000; its readership over 300,000.

Val McCalla launched the *Weekly Journal,* the first national Black broadsheet aimed at African-Caribbean professionals, in April 1992. Circulation has reached 26,000: a 115,000 readership. Anglo-Nigerian journalist, Isabel Appio, who worked on the *Voice* in 1982 at their Mare Street offices but later moved to *Time Out,* has returned to Voice Communications to become the *Journal's* first editor.

To date, there has been no more than four pages of advertising in any one week, mainly from the public sector. Its newly appointed Assistant Advertisement Manager, Ian Benjamin is keen to develop corporate advertisements in the *Weekly Journal.* Apart from Dyke and Dryden Limited, the major Black British manufacturers and distributors of hair and beauty products, and the large American hair and cosmetics companies who place periodic advertisements, private sector advertising had been almost non-existent. It is only within the last year or so that we are starting to see several full page and double page advertisement from large music companies, car manufacturers, tele-communications companies, department stores and supermarkets, mostly in the *Voice.* So at last attitudes appear to be changing, which can only be a good thing for the future of Black-White interaction in Britain and globally.

Head of Advertising Tetteh Kofi is convinced that once advertisers discover the Black spending community they will realise that they can gain from it. For example, he points out, Blacks are 25% more likely to have satellite television and mobile telephones than Whites, adding:

> British Telecom now have a Black family doing a television commercial. Slowly they have started to see a group of people who are a credible market. One campaign the *Weekly Journal* ran for BT was 'Call Waiting'. There was 25% more response in the *Weekly Journal* than in the *Telegraph* on a Saturday. The coupon number at the bottom of the advertisement related to the source so BT could monitor response.

Kofi pointed out some of the difficulties he had to tackle before getting anywhere with major advertisers:

> During the period leading up to BT privatisation I even wrote a letter to John Major. Black people pay taxes, are part of the British population and should be given the opportunity to prove their worth. There are two things which get in the way of progress — lack of knowledge of the Black community and certain prejudices.

> There was a situation with myself and Zenith, a major distributor of hi-fi-equipment, at a meeting with a senior member of their staff. The staff member said to me: Black people practically invented music: they spend all their time listening to music, making music, it makes sense to target them, but what if my clients say to me, 'we want shoppers not looters'? The guy is Central Media Director of the biggest buying point in Europe. Deep down in their minds they have certain preconceived notions of what Black people are. I must add that since that incident we have developed better working relations.

Isabel Appio acknowledges that the *Weekly Journal* has set news standards and is setting advertising standards. She added that the paper appeals to the group of people who are most independent and individual in their thinking and most socially and politically aware. She is of the opinion that Black people are progressing in Britain and that the Black British dream will become a reality in about thirty years when, she believes, it will be comparable to the American dream.

Isabel Appio

The *Weekly Journal* is currently the only weekly broadsheet in Britain aimed at West Indian and African professionals. The circulation is 26,000 and readership 104,000. It is one of three titles published by Voice Communications Group. The oldest, the *Voice* has a weekly circulation of 52,000 with 300,000 readership. The third, *Pride Magazine*, was acquired from its founding publishers in 1992 and relaunched.

The *Weekly Journal's* rival was perceived to be the weekly newspaper, *Black Briton* launched by its publisher, Joe Harker, formerly on the *Voice* staff, in 1991. In a *Guardian* interview, Harker said it was: 'the first newspaper to go for the educated and upward looking Caribbeans. We have captured the hearts and minds of the positive thinking sector of the population.'

No sooner had *Black Briton* hit the news stands than Voice Communications launched its *Weekly Journal*. On June 26, 1992, two months after the *Journal's* launch, under the headline, CREDITORS CALLED IN TO TROUBLED BLACK TABLOID NEWSPAPER, *Voice* carried a story by their reporter, David Hutchinson, announcing that '*Black Briton* ceases publication'.

One conspiracy theory is that the *Weekly Journal* helped to kill off *Black Briton* in its infancy. Certainly, where the bottom line in business is 'dog-eat-dog' there are bound to be casualties. Of *Black Briton's* demise, Hutchinson quotes Val McCalla, owner of the *Weekly Journal*, as saying:

> It's always sad to see any Black business collapsing because I think more Black enterprise should be encouraged... but publishing is a highly risky and difficult business which unfortunately Mr Harker has learnt to his cost.

A recent addition to the Black Press is *Savoir Faire*. It was launched in August 1994 by Alan Thompson and Azania B, publisher and editor of a sister glossy fashion monthly, *Visions In Black*. The paper is published bi-weekly and has been described by its owners as a newszine — a cross between a newspaper and a magazine. Its editorial office is in Hans

Crescent, Knightsbridge, with other offices at Kings Cross. *Savoir Faire's* editor-in-chief is Selby McLeod, who described it like this:

> This offers the substance of a newspaper with the flair of a magazine; creating the ultimate reader-friendly publication... The concept was borne of the minds of our board of directors, who became dissatisfied with the current crop of publications, both Black and White, whose pages have consistently been dominated by negativity and crass undignified images of Black people. We came to the decision to offer the consumers an alternative, so that if nothing else, the readers out there irrespective of colour, would have an opportunity to see Black people represented as they should be; that is as an immensely talented people, blessed with the creativity, style, dignity and determination to succeed at every endeavour...

The director of the company, Alan Thompson says: 'We started *Savoir Faire* and *Visions In Black* to shed a positive light on Black people.'

It is only recently that the few independently-owned West Indian newspaper publishers have begun to achieve an element of economic success. For example, the *Voice* can now pay its staff realistic salaries and is far removed from the days when Black publishers were forced to move from one printer to the next to keep their newspapers and journals in print. Nevertheless, many West Indian newspapers and periodicals have no sooner emerged than they disappear, and many are still struggling to survive. In the last ten years, many newspapers and magazines have disappeared without trace, leaving a trail of hefty printing bills, unpaid salaries and bounced cheques. When the *West Indian World* went into liquidation in 1985, it left a mangled trail of financial debts and employment grievances. Editor Alfred Tang Chow took the staff grievances to the National Union of Journalists; with the result that the newspaper was blacklisted by the NUJ and its publisher, Caudley George blocked from further attempts at publishing under the title.

Questions can be asked about how commercially viable certain Black newspapers are and how successful in appealing to the masses — and about the extent to which they do make an impact and a difference to society. The circulation figures of the few which are monitored by the Audit Bureau of Circulation are reasonably high, whereas those of some of the unaudited ones are highly suspect. Beulah Ainley, a former executive member of the National Union of Journalists' Race Relations Working Party, said that:

> If you go outside certain Town Halls on certain days of the week you will find piles of certain newspapers just dumped there.

Most newspapers have a cover price and the distribution to the newsagents would normally be handled by the large distributors — also at a price. However, it is newspaper proprietors' prerogative to decide whether they want to provide free copies of newspapers at town hall foyers. If this method of media promotion attracts lucrative local authority advertising then no doubt it is worthwhile.

The London-based edition of Africa's flagship journal, *West Africa* relocated to Camberwell, South London, in 1987. The journal was founded in Africa in 1917 under a very different regime and is one of the oldest African news organs published in Britain. It was once owned by Cecil King's Mirror Group but was bought by the South African Government in 1978. Nigeria objected so strongly to the apartheid regime owning the paper that it forced its sale to the *Daily Times of Nigeria*, owned by the Nigerian government. The Federal Government of Nigeria now owns sixty percent of the company.

Editorially *West Africa* focuses on economic and political issues pertaining to the African continent and has been Africa's most authoritative weekly for over seventy-five years. Foreign editions appear in Britain, Austria, Ghana, Sweden, Belgium, Liberia, Switzerland, Canada, the Netherlands, Gambia, Sierra Leone, Germany and the United States — wherever there is a high concentration of African nationals.

Also Nigerian owned is Chief Abiola's *Concord* newspaper. Abiola is a multimillionaire who has been embroiled in political controversy and recently imprisoned for allegedly declaring himself president, after winning a majority of votes in Nigeria's last elections. *Concord* has since been banned in Nigeria.

Nobel Laureate Wole Soyinka protested that 'the election was fair, accepted internally and externally as a marvellous moment of nationhood for Nigeria. It is a mandate that I believe we are defending'. And reacting to the recent clampdown of the media, Ladi Lawal, the newly elected president of the Nigerian Union of Journalists, has appealed to the government to lift its ban on certain publications, including all those in Abiola's Concond Group (*Voice*, 26.7.94).

Africa World Review, a 60-page journal, was launched in April 1991, in order, according to its marketing spokesperson: 'to transcend the cynicism and pessimism that saturates media coverage and academic discourse on Africa.' It is said to provide a point of contact for Pan-African activitists and it focuses on human rights, political and cultural issues.

The most dynamic figure in modern African journalism was Dr Nnamdi Azikiwe, Nigeria's first president. He was educated at a segregated college in America and spent some time in Britain. He returned to Africa and started the *West African Pilot* and at one time owned six titles. Papers that are owned by Africans continue to sustain their following in Britain.

Chapter 9

THE MAGAZINES

The African-Caribbean magazines fall into several categories. There are the women's magazines: *Pride, Black Beauty and Hair* and *Candace,* and the fashion glossy, *Visions In Black.* There are special interest magazines: the political *Race and Class,* the multicultural magazines *New Impact* and *Wasafari*, and the arts and entertainment magazine *Artrage.* There are also several religious magazines and sports magazines.

The oldest is *Race and Class*, which appeals to a multiracial readership with an interest in Black issues in Britain, Europe and developing countries. It was founded 20 years ago by Sivanandan, a Sri Lankan academic. It is a quarterly, pocket-sized academic and political journal with a circulation, mainly on subscription, of 3,500 per quarter. The *Black Parliamentarian* celebrated the election of four Black MPs to the House of Commons in 1989.

Caribbean World is a quarterly magazine promoting the Caribbean as a holiday destination. It is aimed at 'professionals at the upper end of the ABC1 market and provides readers with comprehensive historical background to the countries it promotes'. Its publisher is Ray Carmen.

Black Enterprise was one of several journals created to meet the new entrepreneurial culture, and the needs of self-employed Black people. *Body Politic* is the Black voyeurs' answer to porno-erotica. It is a 50-page quarterly, edited by Elsie Owusu. She says she wants it to be popular but not populist. 'It is meant to be a journal, but then again it's not trying to be a *Cosmopolitan* or *Company*'. Launched in the summer of 1993, it costs £2.95. The writers use pen names like 'Love', 'Grace', 'Q' and 'Lau'. The magazine highlights alternative sex and dressing and the advertising could be judged as bizarre as the editorial contents. One double-spread for example show two mummified images swathed in bandage, one holding out a well-known credit card. Editorially the magazine gives a lot of space to pornographic images and contents. Under the heading: THREE SIDES TO PORNOGRAPHY, a writer dives into a three-sided debate for and against pornography. The magazine tries to straighten its strong porno-bent by attempting three short and shallow political features: one on Prince Charles and Princess Diana, one on Winnie Mandela and one on Ken Livingstone.

Pride Magazine is a relaunch of the old *Pride*. It was acquired by Val McCalla from its founder-publishers, three young North-West Londoners who had to sell it for financial reasons. It is now targeted at 'the woman of colour' in the 18 to 35 age group. Since its relaunch in February 1993, the circulation has jumped to 40,000 per month. Voice Communications' Group Marketing Director, Tetteh Kofi has since launched the magazine in Ghana, Germany, Holland, Jamaica, Canada, and North America and it is now poised to go into the new South Africa.

Pride showed great promise in the first few months of its primary launch. Its founding team produced stories that were controversial, original and of historical interest. The first issue made national news

Deidre Forbes
Credit: Colin Patterson

headlines with its story that the composer Beethoven was Black. Shabaz Lamumba, the researcher who broke the story, quoted German anthropologist Frederick Hertz, who is said to have identified Beethoven's 'negroid traits, his dark skin and flat nose'. He argued that portraits and illustrations of Beethoven by Ferdinand Schimons (1819) show features and traits not associated with Caucasians.

Now that *Pride* is under new management, it will be interesting to see which way it will go. Since its relaunch, it has moved away from being a general interest magazine to becoming a women's magazine. In the 1980s, the Voice Communications Group had launched *Chic*, a glossy women's general interest magazine, not dissimilar to *Pride*. It was once edited by Winsome Cornish, now *Voice* managing editor. Its features editor was Brenda Emmanus, currently presenter on the BBC 'Clothes Show'. *Chic* was eventually sold to Nigerian publisher, Eddie Eroh, then based in Docklands. It has since folded. *Pride's* editor, Deidre Forbes, is the former arts and entertainment editor on *The Voice*.

An African-Caribbean woman, Rasheeda Ashanti, founded *Wadada*, which ran from 1981 to 1986. It was a bi-monthly educational magazine targeted at schools and funded by Hammersmith and Fulham Council. In 1989 she replaced it with *Candace*, the magazine which in many ways most reflects the African image. Ashanti told me:

> Judging by the letters and requests I started getting, readers — mainly parents and teachers — told me that they wanted a general interest magazine. That's why *Candace* was brought out to replace *Wadada*.

Brenda Emmanus
Credit: BBC

Candace was initially funded by the Department of the Environment, to the tune of £4,000 for a pilot run of 5,000 copies to prove its viability. They were sold out within eight weeks. We made £2,000 on the pilot issue.

I went back to the DoE but I don't think they were expecting us to succeed because when I did it was like: 'where shall we send her now?' They sent me to the Hammersmith Economic Development Unit. EDU sent me to the Black Business Development Association who put together a business plan for me. They had to again put it to the DoE.

It took 18 months to get £10,000 in the form of loans and grants from the pilot issue to the next issue, from the DoE. *Time Out*, the distributors get 50 percent of the cover price of each copy.

Ashanti is proud of the name *Candace*, the highest title given to African women of distinction. She boasts: 'it's as good as saying empress, princess or queen.'

When we saw the niche in the market we realised women were aware of the importance of self-esteem. They were saying 'we deserve more'. They want to look good, they want to read about positive things. Features cover health, body, mind and spirit because we saw the importance of the balance.

Candace covers fashion and beauty, career profile, relationships, the arts, travel, eating out, celebrity inter- views, tips for parenting. It is aimed at the 18 to 40 age group.

Rasheeda Ashanti

According to Ashanti, the magazine makes the company approximately £13,000 every two months, but this barely covers the production costs. There are four full-time staff and several freelance contributors and trainees but she told me that many of them only get expense money. Several readers have also told me that the magazine's publishing is erratic and that I'd be very lucky to see the magazine four times in the year.

A symptom which afflicts most Black periodicals and newspapers is the dearth of advertisements from the commercial and public sector. Ashanti observes that:

> Corporate and public sector advertisers need to be educated that Black people are the largest spenders of cash, because if a Black woman wants to buy a television or a video they cannot get a loan so they have to find the cash.

> Look at expensive perfumes and fashionable clothes. Black people are the greatest spenders but these companies are saying they can reach the Black readers through the *Sun* or the *Mirror*; as though those are the only publications Black people buy.

Candace is distributed in Jamaica and Ghana and is about to be go into Antigua, Nigeria and South Africa.

Hawkers, publishers of *Black Beauty and Hair* have practically cornered the Black hair care readership. The magazine was first published by Reed, IPC's parent company, in 1981, which also published its White people's equivalent, *Hair.* Reed was approached by Black hairdressers and hair-care company representatives who informed them: 'We need our own magazines because Black people on the whole cannot relate to *Hair.*'

Black Beauty and Hair changed ownership in 1987 when Reed sold to an Asian Zimbabwean, Pat Petker and a White Kenyan, Richard Hawkins, who are both former Haymarket Publishing professionals. Between them they control several titles under the parent company, Hawker Publishing, three of which target Black readership .

Hawkers also publishes the annual *Black Hair Style*, 'a manual of new hair trends and old classics', according to *Black Beauty and Hair's* editor, Irene Shelley. 'It's a guide for people who need ideas so the hairdressers who are the subscribers, or the consumers, can take it to the salon and show it.'

A third title, *Bridal Issue,* is aimed at the Black bridal market: it covers bridalwear, hair ideas, cooking, traditional and 'modern marriage tips and ideas that the Afro-Caribbean market wouldn't find in other publications,' says Shelley.

Irene Shelley has been editor on *Black Beauty and Hair* since 1987. Born in Nigeria but growing up in Britain since she was three, she comes from a fashion background. She studied at Ravensbourne College and for an MA degree at St Martins College, London. She later landed a job as fashion editor on *Root Magazine* in the mid-1980s, which lasted two years until *Root* was sold to Hansib Publishing. '*Black Beauty and Hair's* circulation has increased by a quarter since I've been here', she says. It's now 21,000 sales and 200,000 readership. The core age group is from 18-35, but, she says:

> We get school kids reading us, we get grandmothers reading us. It's mostly sold in the UK but we have subscribers all over the world and a distribution of 2,000 in Holland.

Editorially, *BB&H* focuses on features covering beauty trends, new salons, new products, how to take care of the hair, celebrity profiling and sociological issues such as the political correctness of perming. There's a big debate about 'are you selling out if you straighten or perm your hair with chemicals?'

BB&H is aimed specifically at women but men feel excluded because they take equal care of their hair. Shelley explains:

> It's editorial policy to keep it to our target readership, so if you open up the magazine to the celebrity profile section you won't find any article on male pop stars, because it's an editorial policy.
>
> I don't see us changing drastically because it's the sort of information people can't find anywhere else so we'll carry on as we

are. I don't think the readers want us to change necessarily. However, we are trying to introduce a round-up of what goes on in the rest of the world; more styles and ideas from Africa, America and Europe.

BB& H is a quarterly magazine and its writers and contributors are all freelances, 'some from the nationals', according to its editor, 'regular writers from the *Guardian* and the BBC for example.'

The first Black-owned fashion magazine to appear on the market was *Visions In Black*, founded in 1993 by Alan Thompson, amidst much controversy. It is a bi-monthly glossy magazine geared towards the ABC1s. It regularly features top designers such as Lacroix, Vivienne Westwood, Karl Lagerfeld, Yves Saint Laurent and Paco Rabanne, and some of the alternative ready-to-wear designs such as Red or Dead and Joe Casely-Hayford. It is the newest African-Caribbean glossy on the market and the only one specifically geared towards high fashion.

At first it was criticised for trying to copy *Vogue*, beginning as it did as *Vogue In Black*. Indeed many people assumed that it was somehow connected with *Vogue* Magazine. But as soon as *Vogue In Black* reached the news stands, it was forced off. As to be expected, *Vogue* Magazine took exception to the use of the name without their consent. Alan Thompson ended up in court over the matter and was compelled to make an expensive U-turn and a sudden magazine name-change to *Visions In Black*.

Irene Shelley

There was a gap of several months between the first issue of *Visions In Black* appearing in the shops and the second, which lead many to believe that the magazine had folded. I asked Alan Thompson the reason for this and he replied that they sold 27,000 copies of the magazine within 14 days, out of the 30,000 copies distributed from the first print run. He explains that the remainder of unsold copies had to be withdrawn from the shelves due to the circumstances leading to the Court action.

According to Thompson, *Visions in Black* is aimed at the 18-45 age group and distributed in America and South Africa in addition to Europe.

Black artists and performers have made huge contributions to popular art and entertainment globally. Yet only a handful of magazines specifically target that market. *Artrage* was launched more than ten years ago by a group of artists and performers and came out of the Minority Arts Advisory Service (MAAS), a voluntary organisation set up by an Asian woman, Naseem Khan, to carry out research into the arts scene in Britain in the 1960s. Much of her research was concerned with the mainstream attitude to minority arts — *The Arts Britain Ignores*, as she called her book. MAAS also operated as a centre for support and to represent non-Europeans. It provided a list of performing and creative artists, for consultation by schools and local authorities.

MAAS did a good job in terms of advocacy and campaigning and it was later felt that they needed a media outlet to articulate the views of the Black artists in all fields, creative and performance, who used the centre. Hence the title: *Artrage*.

The current managing editor, Jacob Ross informs me:

> It is quite unique as a Black media organ as it is the only one that has given a platform to people in the arts who have important views on aesthetics and about the issues that affect artists generally.

> The magazine has always had tremendous prestige and, as a matter of fact, there came a point when one kind of major achievement for these artists was to be featured in it. The major artistic innovators have all been featured in *Artrage*.

MAAS has been financed by the Arts Council, Greater London Arts and the London Boroughs Grants Units and *Artrage* has never been a profit-making publication. So it has a culture and a whole way of thinking which is anti-commercial. 'We have only just begun to posture as a commercial magazine,' says Ross. It has a board of management and a financial structure whereby core staff are paid.

Artrage has never had such things as a marketing and promotions budget but was launched as a magazine which had complementary items for the thousands of subscribers who were members of MAAS. Of the 10,000 copies printed each month, fifteen percent go to the regions and seventy percent to London. The rest is shared between Europe and the rest of the world through a mail-out system to subscribers in places as far afield as Norway and the United States. Ross told me:

> *Artrage* has its own distribution network; the subscribers are the Arts Council, the regional arts authorities, universities, colleges, libraries, its thousands of artists members and supporters, in Britain and around the globe. More than 82 percent of the magazine is sold out within the first three weeks.

Jacob Ross took over as editor of *Artrage* five years ago after moving from listings magazine *Black Arts in London*, which he edited for as many years. When I asked Ross whether he was happy with *Artrage* editorially when he took over, he replied:

> I did not like what was happening with the magazine; I thought it was an internalised piece of intellectual w...ing. But there were a couple of people whose work I respected, people like Archie Malcolm, a former editor on the magazine. Julian Brutus, the editor before me, came in at an unfortunate time when the organisation was going through radical changes.

Artrage started life at 25 Tavistock Place, London; moved to Shackle-well Lane in East London in the late-1980s and to Brixton in 1994. Since then the name of the voluntary unit has been changed from MAAS to Artrage Inter-Cultural Development Agency — shortened to Artrage Agency. 'One has moved away from calling oneself a minority. I mean, what is ethnic? What is minority?' asks Ross.

Jacob Ross was born in Grenada, an academic and ex-Minister of Cultural Affairs in the Grenadian government. But he was quick to point out that 'My background was policy making rather than political'. Although reluctant to discuss politics, he was ready to talk about his academic background. He trained as a linguist and spent most of his academic years in France. 'Presently I'm writing a doctorate on Creole linguistics in my country, Grenada', he says.

Ross's involvement with the media began when he came to London and got involved in the Arts Media Group, a voluntary agency funded by the GLC, which was a support group for Black people in the media.

> For reasons better known to themselves, they shut the agency down and I suppose they thought they'd find me quite useful so they shifted me to MAAS.

There has long been a feeling that as soon as certain Black professional organisations achieve an element of success in campaigning, they are disbanded, and I asked Ross for his views. He did not answer my question directly, but this is what he says:

> I have heard from reliable sources that there is one producer who said that as long as he worked in that national station, there is never going to be a Black face fronting his programme. That's the attitude you get among some of them.

> You will know as I do about the print media as well. I have a lot of connections in the print media and particularly the mainstream print media; it's very incestuous, it's very tight. They hardly ever advertise their jobs, a lot of it is based on the friendship network, a lot of it is based on who you know.

> Speaking as a cultural anthropologist as well, popular culture is Black culture: the music, the clothes, even the way the kids walk. In the word of one Black American: 'the world dance to our music.'

> *Artrage* is a unique resource, it's a massive responsibility and I am committed to its success. We've been given a brief to produce this magazine and we have to make it sell now, whereas before we didn't

have to think commercially. It has been going for a very long time and I have no doubt it can continue to survive...

My idea of the new-look magazine is that it should be a good looking product. Within it you have articles which the students in colleges, for example, doing a degree in media studies or in art development, or arts aesthetics or whatever, can go through it and say, 'I want this, I'll photocopy it' because it's telling them something about themselves or about their experience in their particular time.

If you want to know where the next gig is, the latest record, radio and television listings, it's here and in addition we carry serious features.

The old *Artrage* was more features and interviews based and Ross spoke of the days of: 'the wonderful interviews with Toni Morrison and Derek Wallcott'. He remembered how 'they predicted in one issue of the magazine that Derek Wallcott would get the Nobel Prize for literature, and he did'.

The new-look *Artrage* is more oriented to events in the arts. Jacob Ross describes the writers and sub-editors on the magazine as 'a very dynamic group of young people'. All are unpaid freelances. Some are arts and journalism students from university, there as part of a work placement scheme, and they edit various sections of the magazine. They meet regularly for editorial briefings with Ross and discuss ideas for the magazine.

A lot of young people 'cut their journalism teeth' with us and then move on and that's great. Dionne St. Hill, who does the *Voice* media section, for example, did her placement here.

This is a good time for *Artrage*, a lot of our subscribers now are young White people. They are in essence the major consumers of Black culture. They are the ones that buy the Michael Jackson albums and go to the pop concerts. If we are talking about really being serious we can do very well commercially.

But although *Artrage* is unique in one sense, there are other Black papers such as the *Voice* which devote a large section to arts and media. The recently launched *Newszine* has incorporated culture, music art and entertainment. The *Voice* has also started to produce a weekly television and radio listings, something which *Artrage* had already been doing. Ross comments:

> There is a slot for specialist magazines and we only happen to occupy one slot. I love competition, but when people begin to mess about and tend to want to assume that they are the only ones who have a right to survive and have a tendency to want to crush other people, then I have problems with that and I rise to that kind of challenge. There is room for all of us.

One begins to read between the lines of Ross's argument as he continues on the subject of media competition:

> Business is a very strange thing, we have to learn to work together in a way that is spiritually supportive rather than seeing every kind of new venture as a threat and as a consequence try to crush it. It's an indication of insecurity and it doesn't say much for the people who try to do that.

> Take a newspaper like *Black Briton*, there was room for that and there is room for the *Voice* and many more like them; competition helps to raise standards.

> What is important for us in the 1990s is that we recognise the fact that we as Black people in Britain have always had a strong media history. One of the first manifestations of this Black media presence was since Claudia Jones came with the *West Indian Gazette*. We have always had an instinct, we have always had a knowledge that we need that kind of a voice.

> She also played a major role in keeping Carnival going, knowing that we can explain ourselves best through our cultural manifestations and also through the fact that we have a voice. It's a tradition that is honourable, it's noble, it goes beyond money because it is to do with not allowing ourselves to be silent or else we'll get trampled on.

In the 1990s there's a lot to be done, there's always a ground-swell for Black publications but they don't survive very often because they fail to move with the times. I will always commend the *Voice,* with its ability to go with the flow. Val McCalla was the first to recognise that there was a growing population of Black Britons who didn't want to hear too much about 'back home' because there was no going 'back home'.

But there are no comparisons with *Artrage.* When you take it to the United States people are asking where they can get it. There are a large number of American subscribers on our mailing list, we are a highly respected magazine, we have a massive network. We also have 67 writers world-wide.

Chapter 10

THE AMERICAN CONNECTION

The Chicago-based *Ebony Magazine* does particularly well, competing with the British Black glossies. *Ebony* preceded the *Negro Digest* which came out in 1942 with a circulation of 50,000, and more than doubled by 1943. Ebony's first run of 25,000 was sold out within hours of hitting the news stands. Today *Ebony's* circulation is two million and the readership nine million. John H. Johnson founded *Ebony Magazine*, a lifestyle glossy aimed at Black America, fifty years ago. Its success story is an inspiration for potential Black newspaper and magazine publishing in Britain. Today *Ebony Magazine*, sold to millions in America and around the world, attracts pages of full-colour advertisements. In a two hundred and twenty-four page magazine, for example, there are more than one hundred and twenty-six pages of advertisements, over a third in all. It has clearly won the confidence of White American businesses and advertisers.

Ebony has dominated the Black glossy market in America for fifty years and has been popular in Britain since the 1960s. Johnson's *Ebony* is said to have helped to redefine Black America and has redefined Black people's image in the eyes of Whites and the rest of the world.

In its editorial themes and contents, *Ebony* successfully provides readers with insight into a wider range of professional contributions and social issues relating to the community it serves. It broadened its readership market so that it transcends age and social group, although it largely appeals to middle-class professionals. It displays role models before its readers as a symbol of Black success and to a certain extent, this also appeals to the lower end of the social scale, offering inspiration and hope. Its marketing department presents it as 'a family magazine with something for everyone. It is intended to mirror the positive side of Black life and Black achievements.'

Ebony's editorial formula has worked from the beginning and after half a century it remains one of the most respected Black glossy magazines. Its unique approach has managed to incorporate a whole range of issues and features that makes it attractive to a much broader audience in terms of both age range and socio-economic group.

Johnson Publishing later launched a pocket-sized news weekly, *Jet*. Sales increased rapidly to 300,000 copies a week. Today, its circulation is nearly one million, making it the largest selling Black news magazine in the world.

Johnson's equivalent male lifestyle glossy, *Ebony Man (EM)*, was launched in 1985 as 'a new magazine with a new message for a new (Black) man.' *EM* features men's fashions, grooming and fitness and general interest. It is the newest of Johnson's titles, with a growing circulation of 250,000.

Black publishing has helped to bring the Black consumer market to the attention of the world of business and advertising. Black newspaper and periodical publishing in Britain is not exactly light years behind our American counterparts but we do have some catching up to do. Arif Ali has been publishing constantly in the community for over twenty years and Val McCalla for over ten. They control a market untapped by White publishers and advertisers. *Caribbean Times'* editor, Mike Massive believes that McCalla in the *Voice*, perhaps more than Arif, has drawn attention to the fact that Black people are at the cutting edge in culture, popular and political life. Things we see on an everyday basis: fashion, popular culture, art, music, forms what young people actualise themselves to. And it works because the paper sells. Today both White people and Black read the *Voice*. Companies like hi-fi manufacturers have begun advertising in the *Voice* and, to a lesser extent, in the *Weekly Journal* — which is a start.

Comparing the British Black glossy magazines with our American counterparts, we can see why some do better than others. Take for instance magazines such as *Essence*, an American monthly lifestyle magazine; *Class*, an American import with editorial offices in London and the United States, and *Pride Magazine*, a Voice Communications publication with overseas distributions. *Ebony's* success is unrivalled, both in terms of readership figures and ability to attract corporate advertising. The American magazines win hands down because they are at an advantage in terms of the number of years they have had to get it right. Secondly, their readership outstrips ours by millions and this pleases the ad-men who reward them with lucrative advertisements. In the next decade things should improve for the Black British press as the European trade agreement takes effect and Blacks in Britain and other parts of Europe realise their inter-European marketing potential.

Ken Campbell, a senior journalist at Hansib Publishing believes that:

> The influence of Americans give people the realisation of what can be achieved, for example, Johnson's *Ebony/Jet* empire. It helps journalists in Britain enormously and it is no coincidence either that Blacks from the Caribbean have similar historical backgrounds so, similarly, we chronicle our own story and how it reflects us in Britain.

> One could also say that in Britain, Claudia Jones and Harold Moody were among the first to identify our community, whereby we can have a social cohesion. They tried to speak to the community.

What the current British-based glossies have failed to do is to recognise the contributions made by key figures in the wider Black community and by historical figures. Instead they have limited their efforts mainly to news and features largely about contemporary Black entertainment and fashion trends. They have largely omitted stories dealing with Black people's contributions, experiences and achievements on a wider scale, so fail to strike a balance between the show business type stories and other positive Black features. Whereas the editorial themes and contents of American imports like *Ebony* have successfully provided readers with a broader insight into a wider range of professional, historical, political and cultural contributions and issues pertaining to the community they serve.

Britain's Black consumers are as sophisticated as their American counterparts. The question arises whether any of the African-Caribbean glossies on the British market will change editorial course and direct their efforts to creating a magazine which appeals to a wide social group and a wider age group, or whether totally new and different magazines which provide that balance will appear on our news stands. Blacks in Britain need to be informed about the modern as well as the historical. If we are going to be critical of the White media's exclusion of Black features and stories from their media airwaves and their news pages then it is important for Black publishers and broadcasters in the Black community to lead the way in recognising the Black community in its entirety. If journalists who work in the Black-owned media organisations are prepared to set the media trend in featuring a more balanced perspective of the Black experience and achievements, the White media might well begin to understand and implement changes within their own organisations at a more radical pace rather than as a token gesture.

Britain still appears to be some ten years behind America in magazine publishing but it is making ground. We will continue to see newspapers and magazines emerge and then disappear without trace — Black and White alike — but in a multi-media age that operates on competition and profit African-Caribbean publishers are now cornering a market. But, as one observer says, 'there is room for many more Black media organs' because the competition will in the long run improve standards.

A pan-European Black media will be an interesting development, once the problem of language and other finer points have been tackled. Back in 1918, Marcus Garvey's *Negro World* was published in three languages, French, Spanish and English and although banned in many colonies it was the most popular Black newspaper of its time, read by the millions of members of the United Negro Improvement Association world-wide. As the EU becomes more relevant, the hope is that the potential Black publishing market within the Union and the rest of the Black world will develop into a powerful market force.

Chapter 11

BLACK BROADCASTING

Before deregulation, broadcasting remained unremittingly under White control. A few token Black programmes were granted air time but Black executives and programme controllers were few and far between.

Most of the Black music on the radio airwaves was provided by pirate radio disc jockeys, all of whom risked prosecution and confiscation of their equipment each time they went on air. The presentation was, more often than not, less than professional, but there was a ready market out there, hungry for music and news with a Black perspective.

For the first time in 1989, Black people in Britain were able to bid for a licence to legally own and, within Home Office guidelines, control broadcasting stations.

WNK Radio (interpreted as Wicked Neutral and Kicking) was the only Black pirate station to succeed in their bid for a licence. They went on air in 1990, broadcasting from their station in Wood Green. But they went silent in 1994. WNK's founder and Managing Director, Joe Douglas was unsuccessful in his bid for a renewal of the licence after the four year period expired and WNK went off the airwaves in the summer of 1994. It had shared the licence on the FM waveband with *London Greek Radio* (*LGR*), alternating for four-hour periods daily, twenty-four hours a day. But in the renewal bid, *LGR* were the successful recipients of a new licence and *WNK* lost out.

Today there are only three broadcasting stations which specifically target the African-Caribbean audience: the West London-based cable television station, *Identity Television (IDTV)*, which broadcasts eighteen hours a day; and two radio stations: the Brixton-based 24 hour music station, *Choice FM*, and the Manchester-based community station founded by Mike Shaft, *Sunset Radio*.

Choice FM went on air in March 1990. It is currently the only radio station in London which provides 24 hours of music and a Black perspective. It was formed with a board of six directors, many already established in their own companies. Its target group is ABC1s in the 15 to 35 age group.

Rumours that *Chiltern Radio* had gained controlling interest in *Choice FM* for a sum £250,000 were to prove unfounded. According to *Choice's* Marketing Director, 'three of its directors are also with *Chiltern Radio*, and Colin Mason, Managing and Finance Director, joined the consortium and lent their support.' *Choice FM's* official version of events is that 'Colin Mason, their Finance Director joined the consortium and they have lent their support to *Choice*'.

Choice launched a 24 hour music station in Birmingham on 1st January, 1995. The company has seven directors and a staff of 19 full time and 10 part time in the London office; the Birmingham office is somewhat smaller.

In the Summer of 1994, *Choice* applied to the Radio Authority for a licence to broadcast on one of the new frequencies in order to go London-wide but were turned down. 'The whole idea is to expand the service', said

Neil Kenlock, Choice FM

Kenlock. Nevertheless, their listening audience totals more than 207,000 per week, mainly in the South London area.

Identity Television (*IDTV*) was launched in June 1993 on the London Interconnect cable system, a network which comprises the top five cable systems: United Artists, Videotron, Cable London, Encom and Nynex. It was established by Petra Bernard with two managing directors, Lawrence Nugent and Phillip Ismay. To secure its future success in Europe, they teamed up with the successful Black American cable channel, *Black Entertainment Television* (*BETV*).

IDTVs major backer, BETV was set up in 1980 by American-based Bob Johnson. Today the company is worth nearly $400 million and the 24-hour-a-day station's viewing audience totals approximately 40 million. Johnson, who came to Britain for IDTV's launch, observed that:

> There is a very hungry market for specific programmes for African-British and Caribbean-British people. But nobody is targeting it. *Identity* will attract a loyal following and advertisers will have the chance, just like the *Voice* does, to go to a niche market instead of major TV and news stations. (*Voice*, 17.8.93)

Currently *IDTV* presents eighteen hours of programming daily, between 12pm and 6am, featuring shows from Africa, the Caribbean, the United Kingdom and the United States, aimed at the West Indian and African audience.

On October 1st, 1994, IDTV launched on General Cables' Windsor TV network, bringing its daily potential audience to approximately 800,000 viewers.

Ironically, Black Britons had more Black programmes to choose from in mainstream television broadcasting during the 1980s than at present. Television programmes included 'Black on Black' presented by Trevor Phillips and Beverley Anderson; 'Eastern Eye' presented by Shyama Perera and Samhir Shah; 'Bandung File' presented by Darcus Howe and produced by Tariq Ali and the popular BBC2 series, 'Ebony', put together by a succession of presenters and producers. But by the 1990s, all apart from 'Bandung' were scrapped and none has been replaced.

What was left in terms of home-grown ethnic oriented programmes were two comedy series, 'The Real McCoy' on BBC 2 and 'Desmond's' starring the late Norman Beaton, shown on Channel 4. At a press reception to launch the fifth series, the need for Black comedy shows like 'The Real McCoy' was questioned. One of the actors, Llewella Gideon identified two reasons: there is a real problem about access to television for Black actors and there is also a problem about how Blacks are portrayed. She added, "The Real McCoy' is unique in trying to portray Blacks not as pimps and prostitutes but as human beings'.

There are also the popular American slots, 'You Bet Your Life', a daily quiz show presented by Bill Cosby and shown on Channel 4, and the twice weekly 'Oprah Winfrey Show', first run on Channel 4 but recently acquired for Sky Television in a phenomenal bid.

In the 1980s, the fortnightly magazine programme 'Black on Black' was on air alternate Tuesdays at 11pm, sharing the transmission times with the Asian magazine programme, 'Eastern Eye'. Because it was a late slot — the last of the evening — neither reached its full potential audience.

'Black on Black' was jointly presented by former Oxford headteacher, Beverley Anderson, and Trevor Phillips, a former President of the National Union of Students who also directed and produced the programme, which appeared to be seeking to keep a balance between serious current affairs and light entertainment. But *Race Today*, (October 1984) reported a leaked memorandum from the then executive producer, Jane Hewland to Barry Cox, which suggested that the staff of 'Eastern' and 'Black on Black' 'want out of the television ghetto'. This is apparently how they viewed a situation in which a specialist slot had to be made available for them to utilise their skills.

BBC's Afro-Caribbean Unit at Pebble Mill in Birmingham, from where the weekly magazine programme, 'Ebony' was produced, has been dismantled and incorporated within the Asian Unit. But in a broadcasting environment which is constantly changing, all indications are that the Asian Unit will be replaced by a Multicultural Unit.

In an article in the *Weekly Journal*, Trevor Phillips argues that '...working in one unit does not preclude programming aimed at one minority or another...' and that, '... a Multicultural Unit will help to give voice to the many other minorities — Chinese, Arabs, Central Europeans for example — who would be swamped by the larger minorities.'

Certainly a few Black journalists such as Trevor McDonald, Moira Stuart, Paul Green, Leon Hawthorne and Jacqui Harper have been absorbed into mainstream television as news and current affairs reporters and presenters, but for every four or five Black journalists who have gained entry into mainstream broadcasting there are a dozen more who are excluded and have to be more than persistent in order even to get an interview.

In an interview, Jacqui Harper, who presents BBC's Newsroom South East, spoke about her attempts to get into journalism, and how she:

> ... applied for the BBC's prestigious graduate-entry scheme but was turned down. She laughingly suggests that she could show an entire drawer-full of rejection letters from countless radio and television companies. Jacqui, who was a financial journalist, wrote traffic reports for AA Roadwatch on one occasion to pay the rent. (*VS Magazine*, Aug. 1990).

In 1993 the BBC's Equal Opportunities Department launched *Public Broadcasting For A Multi-Cultural Europe*. The stated aims were to promote the role of public broadcasting in the development of multicultural Europe and to increase the participation of Black and ethnic minority people in broadcasting. It laid out its objectives: to formulate guidelines which enable public broadcasters to avoid negative and stereotypical portrayal of Black and ethnic minority people; to strive towards high quality multicultural mainstream programming which promotes harmonious relations between different ethnic, religious, cultural and linguistic groups; to develop joint strategies for using educational and social action broadcasting as a means of countering racism and xenophobia within Europe; to share good practice in establishing equal employment opportunities within European broadcasting organisations; to establish networks to facilitate all the above.

On June 9, 1993, ninety BBC employees attended a meeting of the newly formed Black support group, the Black Workers Group (BWG). It was established to support Black staff within the BBC, who often find themselves isolated. It has a campaigning role and also provides a platform for discussing employment, programming and editorial issues.

'We need proper representation of the Directorate Implementation Group, to get things done and influence change. I'm very optimistic about the future of the BWG and look forward to positive dialogue in the future', was one representative's reply when asked about the role of the group (*EqualitiTV issue No.7* — Oct. 1993).

Time Out carried a feature under the heading: FOR COLOURED ACTORS AND ACTRESSES WHO HAVE CONSIDERED THAT THEY AIN'T GETTING ENUF back in November 1979. The story was about the portrayal of Blacks in television and on stage and the importation of Americans to play roles which could readily be performed by British artists. Among others, it quoted actors David Yip and Floella Benjamin on the subject, and described Carmen Munroe as 'one of the country's most under-rated actresses'. In the words of *Time Out*: 'Black actors and actresses are getting fed up with being cast as prostitutes, pimps and thieves.'

Floella Benjamin gave an account of her own experience.

I've done three dramatic roles on television this year. In the BBC's 'Waterloo Sunset' and 'Angels', I played a prostitute and in LWT's 'Kids', I played a good time lady who neglects her children. I've said to producers and directors: why can't you give me straight parts? and they reply, 'it's not realistic my love, the public wouldn't accept it'.

More than fifteen years later, one wonders whether much has changed in the way Blacks are portrayed in plays ands films and in the media in general or whether there still remains the problem of stereotypical images, irrespective of achievements. In an interview with Paula Yates on Channel 4's *The Big Breakfast*, as recently as September 7th, 1994, Black supermodel Naomi Campbell told Yates that she had just been asked to play a hooker in an up-coming film. One questions whether Black personalities are really taken seriously by White media owners and controllers. How long will it take before the Black newspapers and magazine publishers and the presence of Black people in radio and television have an impact on Europe, when things are moving so slowly in Britain?

Chapter 12

THE WAY AHEAD

The Black press has an important role in Britain today. Firstly, it sets out to fill the news gap created by the mainstream media's relative exclusion of Blacks from their news-making processes and, secondly, it serves to counter stereotypical images of Black people portrayed by the mainstream media. These images have been increasingly perceived to be counter-productive, however, and we are now beginning to see a breakthrough in the way the mainstream deals with news concerning Blacks. There are now Black journalists, although a disproportionately small number, working in the mainstream media. Thirdly, the Black press provides a training ground and stepping stones for Black journalists, skilling them for jobs as television and radio broadcasters and as newspaper and periodical journalists in the mainstream.

Len Garrison, founder of the Black Cultural Archives in Brixton, argues that the involvement and contributions of hundreds of Black people have been ignored and forgotten and that there is serious omission and neglect of the Black past in documentary history and education and information processes. By the 1780s there were some 15,000 Blacks in Britain. He cites as examples George Bridgetower, professional violinist and a close associate of Beethoven; Ira Aldridge, the actor whose Othello was said to have been unsurpassed on the English stage; Mary Seacole, the Jamaican nurse whose bravery on the battlefields of Balaclava in the Crimean War in 1855 has gone virtually un-remembered. Yet the general media's portrayal of Blacks, particularly of African descent, is that they have criminal tendencies and that the only good thing they are capable of is excelling in sport.

Peter Fryer, in his book, *Staying Power,* gives an absorbing account of the history of Blacks in Britain, and contends that 'Black people have been living in Britain since Roman times but have been excluded from the decision-making processes.' He notes, for example, that the sewing needle was invented by a Black person during Mary I's reign.

Today Britain's Black population stands at over 3 million, most of whom subscribe to at least one media organ, be it television, radio, magazine or newspaper, yet there are still only a few token Blacks employed in the mainstream media. According to research carried out by Manchester University on 'Ethnic Dimensions of the 1991 Census':

> This figure is likely to almost double its current level within a generation. This prediction is based on the age profiles of each constituent group, heavily weighted to the under-20s. Researchers Roger Ballard and Virinder Singh Kalra said that it will be many years before the death rate among ethnic minorities matches the birth rate, so it will grow for many years until it stabilises in a generation (*Guardian* 20.1.94).

Blacks have made vast contributions for many centuries to building up the British Empire. The notorious slave trade funded the wealth that fuelled the Industrial Revolution. The enormous wealth was taken from Africa's natural resources: gold, diamonds and most of its precious minerals. Yet Africans and the descendants of Africans are still marginalised and excluded from decision making processes and key positions in Western society.

In his article in the *Guardian Weekend Magazine* of August 20, 1994, Mike Bygrave observes that 'it is not an idle claim of Anglo-American intellectuals to suggest that slavery lies at the root of modern European and American Worlds.'

Bygrave argues that it is understandable that people of the African diaspora should want to construct an identity that provides pride and security. He quotes Trinidad's former Prime Minister, Eric Williams, when he identified the legacy of slavery as one of the causes that lies at the root of racism. 'Slavery was not born of racism; rather, racism was a consequence of slavery.' Bygrave observes that:

> Slaves, at first called Africans, began to be called 'negroes' and their enslavement justified by their uncivilised subhuman animal-like qualities etc... The whole dreary catalogue of lies, fantasies and guilt we call racism heaved itself into being...The slave trade was abolished in 1807, slavery itself in 1834 — just in time for the British Empire, which needed, and got similar justification in similar terms. Only its geographical reach was wider, for example taking in Indians as well as Africans.

The European countries particularly active in slavery and colonialism were Britain, France, Germany, Italy, Portugal, Spain, The Netherlands and Belgium. In Britain, William Hawkins started to trade humans as slaves from West Africa to the New World in the fourteenth century. He later became Sir Hawkins and his coat of arms is a slave in bondage.

> ...A newspaper called *The Watchman* published an article calling upon the 'friends of humanity to ... pull altogether, until we bring the system (of slavery) down.' The mulatto editor of the paper, Edward Jordon, was arrested and charged with sedition and treason. (*History of Jamaica*).

Compensation money was paid to sugar plantation owners after the abolition of slavery. But the slaves were left penniless. The slave traders received a total compensation of £20m. But slaves were never ever compensated. Today politicians in Britain, Africa and America are calling for compensation money to be paid to the descendants of everyone whose forefathers had been enslaved by the European countries concerned. Organisations such as the Brixton-based World Development Movement is calling for the wiping out of Third World debts. Bernie Grant, Labour MP for Tottenham and an executive member of the European media organisation, SCORE, has won support from various politicians including Chief Abiola, publisher of *Concord* and numerous social thinkers. An umbrella organisation, The Africa Reparations Movement (UK) was launched by Bernie Grant in

December 1993, at a conference sponsored by the Voice Newspaper Group and held in Birmingham, setting out the agenda and objectives for the Movement's campaign.

Broadcaster and journalist Joan Bakewell, in the *Guardian* (21.3.1994) referred to The Africa Reparations Movement and listed some of their objectives:

> ... the return of more than 2,000 Benin Bronzes which were seized by a British naval expedition and which are today held at The British Museum and the Berlin Museum. They are also asking for the cancellation of all Third World debts

> Attempts to control man's inhumanity, laws and conventions are proliferating. But they can't keep pace with the claims of the wretched of the earth. What is certain about any conflict is that when the fighting is over, the claims for redress will only just be beginning.

Today, more than one hundred and fifty years after emancipation, many Black people still feel a sense of injustice because they are still denied equal opportunities in many respects, in spite of their considerable contributions to Western society.

The national media's serious commitment to the Black population will in time contribute to giving the black audience a voice — and value for their money. It will help to ensure that news about Black people which appears in national newspapers and on television and radio becomes more representative of the different communities who subscribe to them.

BSkyB television and ITN still employ only few Blacks whereas Channel Four Television has been exemplary in addressing the issue of ethnic minority broadcasting and seeking to take the Black audience into consideration. Yet 'Desmonds', until December 1994 the only established home grown series left, was axed, although this was due to the ill health of its central character played by Norman Beaton who, tragically, died within weeks.

Attempts were made to contact Farrukh Dhondy for his comment on ethnic minority broadcasting on Channel 4, to no avail. But evidence indicates that Black media workers are more likely than Whites to be representative of Blacks while, still equitably representing the majority White audience. The BBC is now starting to address the issue of equal opportunities but has a long way to go.

The way some of the daily broadsheets present news concerning the different racial groups is also open to criticism. 'Take the Rushdie incident for example' argues Asian journalist, Abdul Montaquin, referring to a march staged by the Muslim community in Spring, 1989, 'under Westminster Bridge there were violent scenes. I saw the treatment they gave Muslims. They did not seek out the true feelings of the Muslim Committee.'

Abdul Montaquin made reference to a story about a Muslim who bought a melon and was reported to have found the name of Allah inscribed inside it.

> The *Independent* gave it a defamatory treatment. The *Guardian* reported it but didn't know what to make of it, so they reported it as a balanced news item which was more sincere.

On the coverage given to a story about two kidnapped babies — one Black, one White — he had this to say:

> One tabloid offered £50,000 reward when Baby Griffiths was abducted. When Baby Glover was abducted, another tabloid offered £5,000. The baby was taken off the 'at risk' register at the time of its abduction and yet the papers carried the story that it was on the 'at risk register. At the first press conference the father was not allowed to attend.

In April 1990, at the age of twenty-one, Abdul Montaquin founded a weekly newspaper, *The Profile*, aimed at young Asians. He received start-up capital from the the Prince's Youth Business Trust, London Enterprise Training Agency, Greater London Enterprise Board and a Midland Bank loan.

Its circulation was 18,000 and it was produced by a staff of five who worked from offices in Docklands. Simon Esterson, a designer on the *Saturday Review* section of *The Times,* designed its pages. 'He gave his graphic design services free of charge.' But the *Profile* folded and Abdul Montaquin now works on the *Weekly Journal.* Tales like these are not unusual.

Generally, the mainstream media have been almost all exclusively staffed by White journalists and mainstream media's owners and controllers have shown little real commitment to employing first level Black journalists such as editors on their staff.

Black people have largely been ignored by the media mainstream except when their stories relate to crime and social unrest. Yet research by the Home Office in 1994 shows that White youth is proportionately more likely to be involved in crime — not a story that was eagerly spread in the media.

The Black media have set a new agenda. They are the voice of Black Britons championing the cause of Blacks past and present. Black newspapers have reported exclusive stories in their newspapers which are later taken up by the national dailies. Black news organs help to draw to the mainstream media's attention stories which might otherwise go unnoticed. Racist perspectives are becoming less generally acceptable in mainstream media. Yet the White controllers and journalists still only rarely consult with the Black communities on issues which concern them and it remains for the Black media to set out to counter the myths.

Newspapers and journals like the *West Indian World*, or *Chic* Magazine, are only a memory now. Numerous others such as *Black Briton , Focus,* a lifestyle magazine from the publishers of the *West Indian World*, *Trade News International* founded by the Gleaner Company, and *Exodus*, a religious magazine founded in the mid-1980s by Movereen Living-stone, all went down within one year. Many observers are closely watching developments in the 1990s between the two main African-Caribbean newspaper publishing companies, McCalla and Ali. Since it is relatively healthy competition, both will probably survive. But there are bound to be other casualties — and many launches of new magazines and newspapers.

Whatever publications emerge and whatever goes under, the impact that the Black press is having on the White media can only grow stronger. By defining a Black readership it has alerted the mainstream press to new market potential. The pressure to change is on, intensified by the visible success of a number of Black people, and underpinned by legislation.

The history of the Black press in Britain is the history of Black struggle world-wide. The first Black-owned papers attacked slavery and its legacy. Then came the long battle to overthrow Imperialism and the rise of organisations like the APU and UNIA, each with its own newspapers and journals to spread the word.

When the issue became discrimination against Blacks in Britain, many of whom had fought as soldiers and seamen for the 'Motherland', these organisations launched publications to take up the cause. And when people arrived from the Caribbean in larger numbers, in response to active recruitment by the British government in the 1950s and '60s, papers appeared for this new readership.

The modern newspapers and journals are part of this proud tradition. They too are organs of resistance, resistance to the exclusion of Black people from power and their omission or stereotyping in the White media. They assert the equal worth of Black people and White. And they create and supply an identified market while also providing the training-ground for Black journalists.

Titles may fail but new ones rise like phoenixes. Every paper, just like its predecessors, speaks to the Black people of the day. Each identifies ideals and observes current trends. The debates about equal rights and Black identity take place on their pages.

It is difficult to predict just how far the mainstream will adapt and include Black people, not only in their daily agenda but also at decision-making levels in production. But the Black press isn't waiting around to see. Fuelled by the memory of the African-American dream and the prospect of a Europe-wide market, the Black press in Britain looks set to serve its public into the next millennium.

Bibliography

Adi, H. (1994) 'West African Students in Britain, 1900-1960: The Politics of Exile', in Killingray, D., (ed) *Africans in Britain*. Frank Cass.

Black, C. (1958) *History of Jamaica*. Collins.

Fryer, P. (1984) *Staying Power: the history of Black people in Britain*. Pluto Press.

Hall, S. (1978) *Policing the Crisis*. MacMillan.

Hall, S. (1991) 'Reconstruction work: images of post-war Black settlement' in *Family Snaps* edited by J. Spence and P. Holland. Virago.

Hinds, Donald (1966) *Journey to an Illusion*. Heinmann.

Jones, C. (1982) *Race and the Media*. Commission for Racial Equality.

Martin, T. (1942) *Marcus Garvey, Hero*. Massachusettes, Majority Press.

Sivanandan, A. (1986) *Asian and Afro-Caribbean Struggles in Britain*. Institute of Race Relations.

MEDIA FILE

Africa World Review, 2nd Floor, 5 Westminster Bridge Road, London SE1 7XW.
0171 620 1430

African Concord, 5-15 Cromer Street, London WC1.
0171 833 4082/3661/5

African News File and Press Service, Euston House, 81 Euston Road, London NW1.
0171 388 0537

African Soccer, Grange House, Highbury Grange, London N5 2QD.
0171 226 8719

African Times, 139 Fonthill Road, London N4.
0171 281 1191

Ahmadiyya Gazette, 8 Haugh Road, Glasgow, G3 8TR.
0141 334 7931

Akhbar-E-Watan, 261 Hoe Street, London E17
0181 521 6630/6634

Al Aalam, 55-57 Banner Street, London EC1Y 8PX.
0171 608 3454

Al Ahram International Newspaper, 107 Fleet Street, London EC4.
0171 583 0692

Al Arab Newspaper, 159 Acre Lane, London SW2.
0171 274 9381 or 737 7733

Al Hawadeth, 183 Askew Road, London W12 9AX.
0181 740 4500

Al Hayat, 66 Hammersmith Road, London W14 8YT.
0171 602 9988

Al Majallah, 184 High Holborn, London, WC1V 7AP.
0171 831 8181

Al Muhajir, 219a Ladbroke Grove, London W10 6HQ.
0181 968 5217

Al Saqi Press, 26 Westbourne Grove, London W2 5RH.
0171 221 9347

Amar Deep, Joyquest Ltd, 2 Chepstow Road, London W7 2BG.
0181 840 3534

Ananda Bazar Patrika and Sunday, 4 Camelite Street, London EC4Y 0BN.
0171 353 1821

Artrage, Lincoln House, 1-3 Brixton Road, London SW9 6DE
0171 735 2062

Asharq Al Awsat, 184 High Holborn, London WClV 7AP.
0171 831 8181

Asian Age, Media Asia Ltd, Suite 4, 55 Park Lane, London WlY 3DS.

Asian Business, 8 Coronet Street, London N1 6HD.
0171 729 5453

Asian Communications, 17a Woodcote Road, Wallington, Surrey, SM6 0LH
0181 773 3773

Asian Express, 211 Piccadilly, London W1V 9LD

Asian Express, First Floor, 35 Piccadilly, London WlV 9PB.
0171 493 8985

Asian Herald, 138, Bilton Road, Middlesex, UB6 8HW.
0181 991 9735

Asian Herald, Room 23, Wickham House, 10 Cleveland Way, London El 4TR.
0181 790 2424

Asian Post, 7 Chicksand Street, London, El 5LD.
0171 377 6764/6754

Asian Times, Tower House, 139 Fonthill Road, London N4 3HF.
0171 291 1191

Asian Trader, 1 Silex Street, London SEl 0DW.
0171 928 1234

Asian Voice, 8 Coronet Street, London Nl 6HD.
0171 729 5453

Asianet Ltd, 525 Great West Road, Hounslow, Middlesex TWS 0BS.
0181 572 7269

Asiavision, Emperor's Gate House, 3 Emperor's Gate, London SW7 4HH.
0171 370 2668

Awaze Aaum, Unit 5B, Booth Street, Smethwick, Birmingham B66 2PF.
0121 555 5921

Bazaar, South Asian Arts Forum, 18 Park Square East, London NWl.
0171 935 9183

Black Beauty and Hair, 140 Battersea Park Road, London SWl l 4NB.
0171 720 2108

Black Enterprise.
0171 928 4090

Black Journalists' Association, 8 Cavaye House, Cavaye Place, London
SW10 9PT.
0171 370 3377

Body Politic, PO Box 2898, London NWl 5RL

Brune, 10 rue Charles Divry, 75014 Paris, France.
(331) 43 95 06 17

Candace, Twilight Publishing, 333 Chiswick High Road, London W4 4HS.
0181 742 8250

Caribbean Times, 139 Fonthill Road, London N4 3HF.
0171 281 1191

Caribbean World.
0171 581 9009 or 0171-729 5453

Choioe FM, 16-18 Trinity Gardens, London SW9 8DP.
0171 738 7969

Cineblitz, 152a Ealing Road, Wembley, Middlesex HA0 4PY.
0181 903 8662

Commonwealth Press Agency Ltd, 290 Pentonville Road, London Nl.
0171 837 2152

Complete Football International, 16 Lanier Road, Hither Green, London SE5

Daily Awaz, Unit K, Middx. Business Centre, Bridge Road, Southall UB2 4AB.
0181 893 5449

Daily Dawn, 62 Milbourne Avenue, Palmers Green, London N13 4SX.
0181 888 7553

Daily Jang, 1 Sanctuary Street, London, SEl lED.
0171 403 4112/5833

Daily Millat, 2 Baynes Close, Enfield, Middx. ENl 4BN.
0181 367 6941

Des Pardes, 8 The Crescent, Southall, Middlesex UB1 lBE.
0181 571 1127

Deshbarta-Eastern News, 170 Brick Lane, London E1 6RU.
0171 377 1584

East African Standard, 11 Holborn Viaduct, London.
0171 489 0063

Eastern Eye, 148 Cambridge Heath Road, London E1 5QJ.
0171 702 8012

Frontline, 300 Westbourne Park Road, London W11 1EH.
0171 221 6490

Garavi Gujarat, 1 Silex Street, London SE1.
0171 261 1527 or 0171 928 1234

Ghana News Agency, 38 Queensgate, London SW7.
0171 581 0228

Gujarat Samachar, 8 Coronet Street, London N1 6HD.
0171 729 5453

Hind Samachar, 478 Lady Margaret Road, Southall, Middlesex UB1 2NW.
0181 575 8694

Identity Television Ltd., 124-128 Barlby Road, Ladbroke Grove W10.
0181 960 3338

Impact International, Suite B, PO Box 2493, 233 Seven Sisters Road, London N4 2BL.
0171 272 8934

India Abroad, Suites 2/3, Stanley House, Wembley, Middx. HA0 4JB.
0181 903 1659/4413

India Mail, 150a Ealing Road, Wembley HA0 4PY.
0181 900 1781

India Times (English), 15 Clement Gardens, Hayes UB3 4AP.
0181 573 5160

India Times (Punjabi/English), 14 South Road, Southall UB1 1RT.
0181 843 1605

India Weekly, 97 London Fruit Exchange, Brushfield Street, London E1 6EP.
0171 377 9969

India-Home and Abroad, 1 Park Close, London NN2 6RQ.
0181 452 4182

Iraqi News Agency, 177 Tottenham Court Road, London W1.
0171 580 6603

Islamic Republic News Agency, Imperial House, 390 High Road, Wembley, Middlesex.
0181 903 5531

Jagaran, 138 Bilton Road, Middx. UB6 8HW.
0181 991 9735

Jamaican Gleaner, 176 Acre Lane, London SW2 5UL.
0171 733 7014

Jana News Agency, 76 Shoe Lane, London EC4.
0171 353 8106 or 8429

Janomot, Unit 2, 20b Spelman Street, London El 5LQ.
0171 377 6032

Journal of Nigerian Affairs, PO Box 246, London SE15 6QS.
0171 252 4669

Kuwaiti News Agency, International Press Centre, Shoe Lane, EC4.
0171 583 2934

Libas International, l0a Berkeley Street, London WlX 5AD.
0171 493 2102

Mashriq, 82 Caledonian Road, London Nl 9DN.
0171 278 3823

Mauritian International, 2a Vant Road, London SW17 8TJ.
0181 767 2439

Mauritius News, 583 Wandsworth Road, London SW8 3JD
0171 498 3066

Middle East Broadcasting Centre, 10 Heathmans Road, Parsons Green, Fulham, London SW6 4TJ

Middle East, I C Publications, 7 Coldbath Square, London EClR 4LQ.
0171 713 7711

Milap Weekly, 56 Broughton Road, London, SW6 2LA.
0171 385 8966

Navin Weekly, 59 Broughton Road, Fulham, London SW6 2LA.
0171 385 8966

Naya Padkar, 7B 1st Floor, Popin Bldg., South Way, Wembley, Midx. HA9 0HB.

New African, 7 Coldbath Square, London EClR 4LQ.
0171 713 7711

New Horizon, ICS House, 144 King's Cross Road, London WClX 9DH.
0171 833 8275

New Impact, AnSer House, PO Box 1448, Marlow, Bucks SL7 3HD.
0628 481581

New Life, 8 Coronet Street, London Nl 6HD.
0171 729 5453

New Patriot, Room 221, Bon Marche Building, 444 Brixton Road, London SW9 8EJ.

New World, 234 Holloway Road, London N7 6NA.
0171 607 6706

News Agency of Nigeria, 44 Grays Inn Road, London WClX.
0171 242 5387

News Watch, 313 Kilburn Lane, London NW9 3EG.
0181 968 6633

NewsAsia, 270 Romford Road, London E7 9HZ.
0181 519 3977

Perdesan Monthly, 478 Lady Margaret Road, Southall, Middlesex UB12NW.
0181 575 8694

Perdesan Weekly,478 Lady Margaret Road, Southall, Middlesex UB 12NW.
0181 575 8694

Pride, 370 Coldharbour Lane, London SW9.
0171 737 7377

Probashi Samachar, 20 Orchard Avenue, London N14 4ND.
0181 886 4231

Punjab Darpan, 2 Chepstow Road, London W7 2BG.
0181 579 2091/840

Punjab Times, 30 Featherstone Road, Southall, Middlesex UB2 SAB.
0181 571 5102/2751

Purbo Desh, Wickham House, Room 23, 10 Cleveland Way, London El.
0171 790 2424

Q News Intemational, Cumberland House, Srubs Lane, London.

Race and Class, Institute of Race Relations, 2 Leeke Street, London WClX 9HS

Ravi Asian News, 123 Grattan Road, Bradford, BDl 2JA.
0274 721227

Sagar Pare, 5 Avondale Crescent, Ilford IG4 5JB
0181 550 4697

Sage Race Relations Abstracts, 28 Banner Street, London ECl.
0171 253 1516

Saudi Press Agency, 18 Cavendish Square, London Wl.
0171 353 7106 or 4465

Savoir Faire, 1st Floor, 50 Hans Crescent, London SWlX 0NA.
0171 713 1828

Sayedatti, 184 High Holborn, London WClV 7AP.
0171 831 8181

Scope Magazine, 5a Westminster Bridge Road, London SEl.
0171 928 3558 or 8108

Seema India News, Sands End Centre, 59-61 Broughton Road, London SW6 2LA.
0171 385 8966

Shafaq, 9 Rockware Avenue, Greenford, Middlesex UB6 0AA.
0181 575 7647

Sikh Courier, 88 Mollison Way, Edgware, Middx. HA8 5QW.
0181 952 1215

Sikh Messenger, 43 Dorset Road, Merton Park, London SWl9 3EZ.
0181 540 4148

Silvarrow, 101 Churchfield Road, London W3 6AH.
0181 933 1740

South Sudan Vision, 77 Levita House, Charlton Street, London NWl lLS.
0171 388 1824

South, Rex House, First Floor, 4-12 Lower Regent Street, London SWlY 4PE.

Spectrum Radio, Endeavour House, North Circular Road, London NW2 lJT.
0181 905 5000

Sri Lankans Monthly, PO Box 110, Edgware, HA8 5RG.
0181 952 9527

Straight-No-Chaser, 43b Coronet Street, London Nl 6HB.
0171 613 1594

Sudan Democratic Gazette, PO Box 2295, London W14 0ND

Sunset Radio, 23 Mount Street, Manchester, M4 4DE.
0161 953 5353

Surma Bengali Newsweekly, 86 Terrace Road, London E13 0PD.
0181 472 0689/0181 981 5571

Surma, 40 Wessex Street, London E2 0LB.
0181 980 5544

T V Asia, T V Asia House, Spring Villa Park, Spring Villa Park Road, Edgware,
Middlesex HA8 7EB

Teamwork, 5 Westminster Bridge Road, London SEl 7XW.
0171 928 7861/2

The Overseas Indian, 5 Hanson Street, London Wl 7LJ.
0171 353 1356

The Punjabi Guardian, 129 Soho Road, Handsworth, Birmingham B21 9ST.
0121 554 3995

The Voice, 370 Coldharbour Lane, London SW9 8PL.
0171 737 7377

The Weekly Journal, 370 Coldharbour Lane, London, SW9 8PL.
071 738 5500

Third World Review, Kwame Nkrumah House, 173 Old Street, EC1.
0171 608 0447

Uganda Review, 7 Thornbury Road, Isleworth, Middx. TW7 4HQ.
Fax: 0181 969 9984

United News of India, 5 Kenton Park Mansions, Kenton Road, Harrow.
0181 907 0592

Urdu Times, 55 Valleyfield Road, London SW16.
0181 677 5353

Visions In Black, 1st Floor, 50 Hans Crescent, London SW1X 0NA.
0171 713 1828

Wasafari, Department of English, Queen Mary & Westfield College, Mile End Road, London E1 4NS

Wasafari, PO Box 195, Canterbury, Kent C/o S. Nesta — Editor

West Africa, 433-445 Coldharbour Lane, London SE5 9NR.
0171 737 2946

West Indian Digest, 139 Fonthill Road, London N4.
0171 281 1191

X-Press, 55 Broadway Market, London E8 4PH.

INDEX